Purring In God's Ears

W. L. Seaver

Paintings by **Jeanne Mack**

Editing and Formatting by www.ChristianEditingServices.com

The front cover: The story of Allie, a diluted calico, is both painful and beautiful. The poise is true to her purring in God's ears. Her story will be in the next book.

To my granddaughters, Paige and Elle, who love my cats;
To friends and colleagues, who love and care for cats;
And to My God, who made such beautiful creatures.

Table of Contents

Preface

Wherever I go and whomever I talk with, I continually find people, children, and adults who are hurting emotionally, mentally, spiritually, and physically. They feel God is far removed from hearing or seeing their circumstances and He is not concerned about them. Such feelings or impressions are natural but totally contrary to what the Bible teaches in Luke's gospel.

"Are not five sparrows sold for two cents? And yet not one of them is forgotten before God. Indeed the very hairs of your head are all numbered. Do not fear; you are of more value than many sparrows." Luke 12:6-7 NASB

Thus, God knows the exact number of hairs on our head, even though that count changes every day or two. So we can be confident God is not distant, but very close to us. He is waiting for us to turn to Him and trust Him with everything.

Several years ago, my family went through a very difficult time. We felt helpless. All we could do was pray, and when we did, God seemed far away and the prayers felt as if they bounced off the heavens. Despite those feelings, I spent a considerable amount of time in a nearby park walking and praying about our circumstances and the people involved. As I walked around praying, I noticed a number of feral (wild) cats in this park. For years they had lived off the scraps on picnic tables and trashcans. But their world turned topsy-turvy when commercialization changes took place. A restaurant opened up and the nearby marina was remodeled, resulting in less food available around picnic areas. Those beautiful and resilient cats were slowly starving to death.

As I observed the struggles of these feral cats on my prayer walks, I realized I couldn't change my difficult circumstances, but I could do something to help them. When I got involved in caring and rescuing the cats, a miraculous realization occurred. First Kings, chapter seventeen, describes a drought that had come on the land of Israel and how God provided for the prophet Elijah during that difficult time. God's provision of water was from the brook Cherith, and God's provision of bread and meat was from the ravens, twice a day. The divine realization in my soul was that I was experiencing my own drought in my heart. I realized I had some misconceptions about God and His ways. God used the cats I was caring for to care for me in this difficult time just as He used the ravens with Elijah. I felt as though the feral cats ministered to me more than I helped them.

As I became acquainted with each cat, their unique purr, and their special story that covers many years, I was inspired to write about them. Bible truths and principles that adults and children could identify with became obvious so I knew I must capture them on paper. Here are just a few of the cats you will be reading about in this book: the cat that lost almost everything he valued, the cat that just wanted a friend (Who can't identify with that?), the cat that nobody wanted, the cat that was considered a mistake, the cat that was a great mother, the cat that was mistreated and abused.

Each true story is related briefly without a lot of needless detail so the reader can identify and understand the unique biblical perspectives and principles throughout the book. The story is always told from the perspective of a cat. Biblical references are not used in the stories, but they can be found in the prologue. In addition, there are colorful illustrations of the actual cats drawn by Jeanne Mack (www.jeanmackart.com) capturing the unique essence of each cat's personality. Special thanks to Jeanne for her passion for cats and her God-given abilities for painting them.

The overall intent of this book is to encourage individuals that God never wastes time or our experiences. Everything that has happened to us throughout our entire life is for our good and the good of others. God promises to work out every situation, good or bad, for our benefit and His honor and glory (Romans 8:28).

When you visit a beautiful municipal, county, or state park, you can't help but be amazed by its beauty. The freedom you sense, solitude you feel, and fresh air you breathe will nourish the soul. However, there is much you cannot see happening in the wildlife natural and unnatural to that area. Many times there are feral cats that have been born in the wild and not tamed by human contact. Some of these animals have been dumped off by people for reasons totally unfair to the cat. Their trust in people has been completely undermined, and they must find a way to survive. Many would see these cats as disposable or nuisances, but the reality is that each cat has a beautiful story to tell. The same is true of people!

As you read my book, I pray you will come away with a favorite story or two you can identify with. I also pray your concept of who God is and what He is like will be expanded, corrected, and refreshed. And lastly, I pray you will see God's hand in the animals around you as well as the people, resulting in praise to God.

CHAPTER 1

Blondie

THE CAT THAT
LOST WHAT HE HAD

When a cat has food, water, shelter, family, love, and safety, he has everything he needs. But what about the feral cat that's living outside and has to brave the elements with danger lurking all around? The poor animal must struggle for survival, which is often a tight walk between life and death. Blondie is my name, and this story is about my struggle.

I am a feral cat living in a spacious park in East Tennessee. My park has about 300 acres for my family to roam around on. I have two brothers, Zeusy and Swirl, and a sister, Shyyell. We are all-American Shorthair cats. I have a half-brother, whose name is Goldie. I think you should know we are not the only feral cat family in our park. At one time there were more than twenty other cats, but enough about my family. I want to get on with my story.

My parents, grandparents, and many generations before them ate the leftover food from the picnic tables and garbage cans. My parents told us they ate very well with all the picnickers once they mastered the tricks of getting in and out of the garbage cans with swinging lids. The getting in was the easy part, but you needed someone to show you how to get out or you could be in serious trouble.

However, over the past few years, there have been some frightening changes around here. There are fewer folks using the picnic tables since the opening of a new restaurant and the remodeling and expanding the marina. This means less food for the cat population and other animals living in this park. As a result, we feral cats are prime targets of the red foxes that roam through our territory.

I thought we were doomed for sure, but a human, whom my parents recognized as someone who walked in the park at least a couple times a day, began leaving food at one or two of the picnic shelters around dusk or shortly thereafter. At first, the food was dry, but later some wet cat food was mixed with the dry. That food was delicious! And occasionally, this human left small morsels of lunchmeat on the dry cat food. Those morsels were my favorite! At first, I wondered if it could be a trap, but the human was never pushy. He left the food and stepped away—he really cared about us and had no agenda.

My parents depended on this once a day meal to survive. As kittens, our parents took us to this picnic shelter so that we could eat too. After tasting the lunchmeat morsels, Zeusy, Swirl, Shyyell, and I couldn't help ourselves. We were so excited to see our new friend that we ran out to him and gobbled the morsels out of his hand. He always had a tidbit for each of us. My dad really liked to meow at him, and the human would talk back softly to my dad and continue feeding us. It was a great cat life!

One day my siblings and I waited for our parents to show up, but they never came. We didn't know what happened to them. Zeusy was sure they died from old age, but I was convinced they were killed by our biggest predator, the red fox. Swirl pointed out they could have been run over by a vehicle barreling down the roads adjacent to the park. We never knew what took them away from us, but we knew they were gone for good.

The winter after our parents disappeared was very cold. We shivered from the frigid temperatures and hated all the snow, ice, and freezing rain. We thought for sure we would starve to death, but the human showed up every day, rain or shine and fed us.

Not long after we lost our parents, Swirl and Shyyell were adopted by a family. So they left us too. The human continued to come. Zeusy was very friendly toward him. Every time Zeusy saw the human, he started purring and even allowed the human to pet him. I took food from the human's hand, but I kept my distance and didn't allow him to pet me.

Our relationship with this human was very interesting over the years. When we heard his familiar whistle, sometimes 400 yards away, we knew he had arrived at one of the picnic shelters. He waited for us, and if we didn't show up right away, he came looking for us. Sometimes when he whistled raccoons showed up, but he chased the raccoons off so we could eat first. Another day when he whistled the red foxes showed up, but they didn't stay long because the main picnic shelter where we ate was covered and had a heavy smell of human scent. This provided a natural protection from the foxes and we appreciated that.

About six months later, the picnic shelter that our parents, grandparents, and many previous generations had fed at was torn down. Again, our environment was changed, but the human was not deterred by these changes. He found other uncovered picnic tables that were close by and placed food on the tabletop, a bench, or under the table. When it rained or snowed, he placed food under the tables on small concrete blocks.

I always marveled at how the human knew just how much food to bring. There was never too much food that would attract predators or too little food for us cats to eat our fill. He always tried to provide exactly what we needed. A few times when he thought we might still be hungry, he would swing back by and give us a little more food. All of us, Zeusy and I, Miss Tort, Goldie, Miss Black, and a tomcat by the name of Gray Boy, were well taken care of at these tables.

Since the new tables didn't have a strong human scent, the foxes were very bold and dangerous. They jumped on the tables and gobbled up any leftover cat food. One time they hopped up where I was eating and bit me in the neck. I luckily escaped, but infection set in my body from my right side, through my shoulder, and up to my ears. I thought I was going to die. I don't know how I had the strength to continue, but I managed to continue going back to where the human was feeding us.

Something strange happened! I noticed the morsels of lunchmeat the human gave me had a slightly different texture. They crunched when I bit into them. Later I discovered he was feeding me medicine with my morsels to get rid of the infection. For eight weeks he faithfully fed me antibiotics in my food. The infection and the wound improved but did not completely heal.

Shortly after the fox attack, the human stopped whistling for us. I knew what he was doing. He was trying to avoid alerting the foxes and raccoons. Instead of whistling, he softly called our names. When we heard his voice, we came out of hiding.

Usually Zeusy and I would always go feed at the same picnic shelter or table. However, I was weakened from the infection not clearing up. I knew any fights with other cats or my own scratching could make it worse. So I went to a table where I was one-on-one with the human. I had my own wet food and my own morsels. No sharing with any other cats. The human showed up with a small cage he would set down and then feed me. Afterward he would take the cage away.

One day he brought the cage (later I found out it is called a trap) and baited it with the lunchmeat morsels. He left the cage and walked away. I followed those morsels into the cage and the door slammed shut. I was trapped and was I ever mad! He picked up the cage, softly called my name, and put me in his car. I was so mad and refused to be comforted by him. He had tricked me and I was scared. That night was the longest night of my life! The fear I felt completely shut down my appetite for food.

The next day he covered the cage with a tarp, placed me in his car, and took me to a veterinarian. I didn't like the place at all! The veterinarian gave me some medicine and cleaned the infection. I felt groggy and was scared I would never see my home, family, and friends again. The human came back and took me to his home for another day, where he fed me and continued to talk softly to me. Just when I didn't think I would ever return home, he took me back to the park and let me go. When that trap door opened, I bolted out of there fast.

The next day I heard him calling my name, but I refused to go. He left some food for me, but I wasn't going to let him trick me again. After a few days, I noticed I was feeling better than I had in a long time. The spring was back in my step. That's the day I realized for the first time that the human was my friend. He wasn't out to hurt me but to help me. I understood why he had trapped me. He was trying to save my life. The next time the human called for me I came running. This time when he fed me, my little heart was overflowing with gratitude. I rolled over and let him scratch my tummy and pet my fur. I realized what Zeusy already knew—this human was our provider, protector, and friend.

After the terrible fox attack, the human found a way to feed all of us cats at the same time in the same location. He was so good at protecting us. And we soon discovered there was less trouble from the foxes when we all ate in the same general area. Our ears were perked up, listening for any predators or people who might harm us. We were convinced the human had brought us together for our own good.

One evening the human showed up, and we were all prancing on our tables, anxiously waiting for food and some attention. Since the fox attack, there was one table Zeusy and I felt especially safe at, but this night Zeusy was crouched in the grass near the edge of the woods. The human called for Zeusy, but he refused to come. The human knew something had to be troubling Zeusy so he walked over to him. Zeusy was in a face-off with a six to eight foot long black rat snake. I had never seen such a big snake. Zeusy wasn't backing down. The snake was poised to strike. The human picked up a stick, stunned the snake, and moved the snake back toward the woods. Later Zeusy and the human went back to check on the snake. They were relieved to discover he had moved on.

In the evening, if Zeusy and I arrived at the tables before the human, I crouched real low in the high grass so only the tips of my ears could be seen. Other times, I hid in the woods until the human showed up and called for me. Just like clockwork, every evening he arrived to feed us. As much as I loved the food, I had to admit I enjoyed the way he talked to us and loved on us even more. He seemed to sense when we were a little jittery and always stayed around while we ate to protect us from the foxes, raccoons, skunks, and snakes, as well as the big bully in our territory—Gray Boy.

Foxes are very sneaky and are rightly called "sly." For instance, a fox would backtrack and show up at the table where we were eating from a totally different direction. Or the fox would bring other foxes with him and come at the table from several directions at the same time. In either situation, the human would flash a bright light in the direction of the fox or foxes to shoo them away. Most of the time, he brought his German Shepherd dog to scare away the unwanted guests.

The human loved us unconditionally! He even made arrangements for other kind folks to feed us when he couldn't come. My friends—Miss Tort, Goldie, and even the bully Gray Boy (who really wasn't my friend since he was always chasing me)—have warmed up to this human and look forward to his visits, his voice, and his love.

One day I heard Zeusy and Miss Tort crying. They had been captured by some park maintenance employees and relocated to another park. I had always warned Zeusy and Miss Tort that their ravenous appetite for food was going to be their downfall and my words came true.

The human kept coming and feeding the remaining cats. One day he sat with me and shared that he thought my brother had been released in another park ten miles away. He promised me he would look for him, but it might take a long time to find him. There was calmness in my heart while with the human, but when he was not around, I was very skittish. He did his best to soothe my fears. I think he could sense how much I missed my brother, friends, and the rest of my family. I was very lonely even though my half-brother Goldie was still around. If it were not for the human, life would not have much purpose! He loved us unconditionally, provided for us, protected us, and spent time with us every day.

Life Values and Lessons from Blondie

1. Blondie was a cat that had it all: great family and friends, great environment, and plenty of food. When he lost his family and friends in various ways, his environment became more hostile and dangerous, and the source of food for his survival became scarce. He lost what he had, but not through what he had done. Sometimes as humans we have to lose everything before we find that Pearl of Great Price, as embodied in Jesus Christ, our Savior and Redeemer.

2. The Unseen One, who sees and knows all, will intervene in our lives when we are helpless and hopeless. He is always there to provide for us, protect us, and lead us.

3. The feral cat world has its dangers: foxes, coyotes, raccoons, vehicles, other cats, snakes, and people. Likewise, there are numerous dangers in the human realm that can destroy our emotional, physical, mental, and spiritual health. However, our God is sufficient to protect and deliver us from them all.

4. On some occasions, the God of the Universe allows us to be wounded emotionally, mentally, physically, or spiritually. The intent of the wounding, which is sometimes life threatening, helps drive us face-to-face to the Healer of all wounds, Jesus Christ. In that daily seeking and meeting encounter, the healing process begins.

5. God's ways to heal our wounds may seem strange, just as it did to Blondie, but His ways are always perfect. We begin our journey of wholeness when our relationship with God the Father is healed through knowing His Son, Jesus.

6. We may lose all we have and value, but when we find our Savior Jesus Christ and He redeems us from all our past, present, and future sins, we have found eternal value and purpose in life.

7. This human loved Blondie unconditionally, and our heavenly Father loves each of us unconditionally. That is why He sent His Son to die for our sin and then raised Him from the dead. There is power in the unconditional love of God, and there is a great joy and peace in knowing His Son as our Friend.

CHAPTER 2

Goldie

THE CAT THAT
WANTED A FRIEND

My name is Goldie. I'm an all-American Shorthair cat, whose name reflects my color. My relatives and previous generations of my family have always lived in the park. I'm a half-brother to Blondie, Zuesy, Shyyell, and Swirl. Even though I am related to these cats, I was never accepted into their circle. They lived in one place and I in another. Their home was under an old merry-go-round in the woods, and mine was close to the marina. Don't get me wrong. We never fought when we met, but they kept to their section of the woods in the park and I kept to mine.

A new restaurant and marina in the park changed the access to easy food at the picnic tables. As a result, my half-brothers Zeusy and Blondie wandered over the entire park looking for food, but I was petrified of the vicious foxes that wouldn't hesitate to corner a single cat and kill him. It was not wise for a cat to roam around the park alone. So my territory of wandering was primarily limited to a section of woods about a hundred yard square next to the lake. My home was a hole in the ground under some shrubbery close to the marina. The smell of boats, gas, and people kept the foxes and other cats from disturbing me.

In the midst of the park changes and turmoil, there was a human who started leaving food around some of the picnic tables every evening. He must have sensed our circumstances and decided to provide food for us. He always fed Zeusy and Blondie first, then Tort and Gray Boy around another table, and then he fed me last. My being fed last was not his fault, but mine. I was always the farthest away from the feeding because of my fears of the other cats—after all, I was the smallest cat in the park. I felt as if I were on the outside looking in as I peeked around trees and spied on him. The human would leave dry and wet food for the other cats, but he always left dry food around the trees for me. The fact that he fed my enemy, Gray Boy, made me realize that he loved all the animals in the park. I'll never forget the moment I was convinced of his concern for each one of us.

During the day I hid in my hole, observed the boats, and enjoyed watching all the people. On one sunny but cool fall afternoon, several ducks were swimming in the water nearby. This was nothing unusual. They did that all the time, especially on warmer days when they wanted to stay out of the way of the boats. There were people watching the ducks and boats, but no one could see me. All of a sudden, one of the ducks began squawking and quacking loudly. The people around the marina just watched and did nothing to help. I looked up and spotted the human who had been feeding us every night and his German Shepherd dog running toward the wailing duck. He tied his dog up, peeled off clothes, and was ready to plunge into the water, but it was too late! The duck had been pulled under the water and never resurfaced. I could tell the human was furious at the bystanders, who did nothing to help. My ears perked up when the human knelt by his dog and told him a big snapping turtle had pulled the duck under. He also whispered how he wished he had gotten there sooner. His deep concern for the duck reinforced the thought that he loved me too.

The human usually fed us after dark and then took his dog for an evening stroll. He would sometimes circle back to make sure we were all right and had enough to eat. On one occasion, after the human fed us and circled back, I was busy eating. I heard some strange noises in the distance. I immediately retreated to the safety of the trees in the woods. The sounds were two foxes sneaking up on us cats from totally different directions. It looked as if one of the cats might be someone's next meal. At just the right moment, the human showed up with his German Shepherd dog, who did not tolerate the foxes messing with us cats. The human released his dog from the leash and those foxes bolted for their lives. The human knew his dog wouldn't catch them, but she could scare them so they wouldn't try such a thing again. He whistled, and the dog returned. We cats and the human knew where the den of the foxes was, and we respectively kept our distance. This was the boldest action the foxes had ever taken against us. I was relieved after the whole ordeal was over, and I heard the human tell his dog, Wiggles, that the foxes may have really been more interested in the cat food than hurting us. I guess we cats weren't the only ones facing hard times. The small animal life in the park was struggling to survive because of the lack of picnic food.

The next night the human left small portions of food, chicken hearts, gizzards, livers, and other odds and ends about 100 yards away from where we cats would eat. Once the foxes discovered this new food, the human fed them and us cats about the same time. The foxes left us alone for a while.

A few months later park employees set some traps in the park. Zuesy, Tort, and Gray Boy were trapped and relocated to another park farther out in the country. I sniffed at the trap, baited with wet cat food. I wasn't accustomed to that type of cuisine. Fortunately, I walked away and didn't get trapped. Before long, it was only Blondie and I left in this section of the park. That made me nervous because of the threats from the foxes.

Now, when the human came in the evening to feed us, there was just Blondie and I. Occasionally, we would see Blackie, who was like a stealth cat and was fed by the human at another location about a half mile away. There were other domesticated cats that showed up for short periods that lived at the park's caretaker's house, but the human generally encouraged them to leave the area because of the foxes.

The human fed us every night. I would never get too close, just peeked around a tree to make sure he was going to leave food. The human sat and talked with us, telling us how beautiful we were, how we needed friends, and how beautiful the evening was no matter what the weather.

For the next year, the routine was feeding us cats in the park and feeding the foxes too. The human never overfed the foxes but left them just enough food so we cats had time to eat and be gone. The human always stood guard with his German Shepherd while we ate. He tried several times over the next year to get close to me, but I was too scared and not very trusting.

One evening, about a year later, just before a bad thunder storm came through the park, the human came to feed us. As was his routine, he fed Blondie and then me. Once we ate, Blondie and I hurried on because the wind, thunder, and rain began. The severe thunderstorm was very frightening! Several big trees crashed to the ground because of the heavy winds and rain. That was a long night! The next evening I was very hungry so I hurried to the place where we were fed. The human was there calling for Blondie and me, but Blondie never showed. Every evening for several weeks, the human called for Blondie and me, but still no Blondie appeared. On one of those evenings after Blondie disappeared, the human told me he was concerned that one of the big trees that fell may have killed Blondie or the foxes finally got him. The human cried for Blondie. I too was very sad since I was more alone that I had ever been. Cats like being alone, but we also like being around other cats. The loneliness was indescribable!

The human continued coming every evening. Our relationship improved, and I really enjoyed the scrumptious meals with chicken and meat. However, while I inched a little closer to the human (for I was very lonely), I kept my distance to about six to ten feet, frequently just peeking around trees. Sometimes the human would pass through the park during the daylight and spot me sunning on the rocks near the lake. He would stop, call my name, and tell me he would see me later that evening. I couldn't help but turn and notice him. It was encouraging for someone to call my name at some time other than the evening.

Some months later in late fall, another cat named Sandy (a Norwegian Forest cat) was dumped in the park. Sandy was yellow and white gold in color with thick fur. He looked to have weighed about sixteen pounds. That was twice as big as I was. I weighed less than eight pounds. Evidently, Sandy had belonged to a family, but he was not woods smart. We met one night, and he followed me to the cat feeding station where the human fed both of us well. Over the next week or so, Sandy would show up about half the time to eat. He was getting too thin! I tried to show him how to hunt and did my best to keep him away from the foxes' territory, but he was not very teachable. He roamed over the entire 300 acres of the park, and frequently came across the foxes. They treed Sandy, and then he would cry for help. When the human whistled, Sandy howled louder. Eventually the human walked through the woods with his German Shepherd and scared the foxes away. This happened several times near the foxes' home in the park, but the human was always there to rescue Sandy.

Finally, Sandy realized he needed to stay out of the fox territory and showed up after dark at the one feeding station, which was rotated in an area to avoid raccoons and foxes. When Sandy showed up every night, we rubbed against each other, rolled around together, played, and ate. I finally had a friend! Sometimes when Sandy was not there, the human roamed through sections of the park whistling for Sandy. The human was not only concerned for Sandy, but he knew the importance of my having a friend. I showed Sandy the safe trails and peaceful sections of the park. I also warned him about the ways of the foxes and taught him how to hunt rabbit, mice, and more. Sandy learned quickly how to survive in the woods.

Every evening after the human fed us and talked to us, he reached out his hand for us to smell his fingers. He was never pushy! An interesting incident occurred when Sandy allowed the human to lightly pet him. Sandy began to purr, something I had not heard since I was a baby kitten. Sandy was very temperamental. Some evenings he would let the human pet him and other nights he wouldn't. One time, Sandy and I were side by side when the human was petting Sandy. Then I allowed the human to pet me. My cautiousness about the unusual human touch caused me to draw back, but inwardly it was a great experience. Over the next week or so, I allowed the human to pet me at the same time with Sandy, and I, too, began to purr. I had found another friend—the human! He had always been there!

On a couple of occasions, another cat passed through our territory. I was too small to fight or tangle with these other cats, but Sandy held his ground and chased them away.

Another time, the foxes approached one of our feeding places, but Sandy stood his ground and I watched his back for another fox from the other direction. The foxes realized they couldn't win this fight. Just as that realization sunk in, the human arrived and the foxes scattered. Afterward, Sandy and I rubbed up against each other. We knew our friendship had become stronger that night! Of course, Sandy was like most friends that can get a little testy every now and then, but we made up quick and it wasn't long before we picked back up where we had left off.

We had a very cold spell for about two weeks so I stayed close to my warm burrow and didn't go to the feeding station. I was very hungry and hunted close to my home. Finally, one evening I heard the human calling my name. When I went out, I found some food at a different spot just waiting for me. As the weather warmed up, I finally returned to the usual feeding station area. Sandy was extremely happy to see me. We rubbed together and played a lot. When the human fed us, Sandy let me eat first since I had not eaten well for two weeks. I heard from the human later that Sandy had not eaten very well in my absence because he missed me. What a true friend!

Sandy and I waited for the human every evening. He fed us, protected us, talked to us, petted us, and continually told us how much he loved us. I looked forward to being with my two friends—Sandy and the human. I never had friends who accepted me unconditionally for who I am. That is something to purr about forever!

Life Values and Lessons from Goldie

1. Goldie had acquaintances but no friends. He always seemed to be on the outside looking in, wanting to belong to the in-group, but the in-group never accepted him. He was a loner, and the loneliness was emotionally painful and physically dangerous. But God, in His great mercy, provided a friend. Better yet, God was his faithful Friend and never left his side.

2. Goldie couldn't do anything in his environment to create friends even as hard as he tried. Maybe it was his size. After all, Goldie was the smallest cat in the park. Maybe the other cats thought he could not contribute or be counted on in a fight for life with the sly foxes. Goldie never knew why the other cats treated him only as an acquaintance and never as a friend. He felt it was something about him that turned the other cats away, and that made Goldie more insecure. However, in the divine scheme of things, God never wastes time or our experiences. He uses everything to accomplish His purposes in a life, even the little insignificant things. For instance, the fact that Goldie was only fed dry food, seemingly a disadvantage, worked for his best when his acquaintances were trapped and relocated. The bait was wet food, which did not tempt Goldie.

3. One of the advantages of always being alone is that one has to develop skills to survive as Goldie did. The knowledge and application of these skills can be a springboard to building friendships in the future. In Goldie's case, these skills were passed on to Sandy to enable him to become woods-smart. The end result of this gentle mentoring of Sandy was the gift of friendship. Sandy was a true friend. Goldie finally had a friend as he gave of himself.

4. In the beginning of the friendship, Sandy didn't have much to give but his presence and company to Goldie. He didn't trust people since he had also been mistreated by them. However, this human was very different! As Sandy became friends with this human, that friendship led Goldie to the unconditional

friendship he had always wanted, the friendship with the human. Friendships should always lead to a deep relationship and trust in the Friend who gave His all for us and desires us to know Him better. As that happens, we can better understand ourselves and where God has placed us.

5. True friendships bring out the best in each other not the worst. Goldie brought out the best in Sandy by giving of himself. Sandy brought out the best in Goldie by helping him in relationships with him and the human. Our friendships, if healthy, should become better, but our relationship with God and our Lord Jesus Christ, our Friend always, should become deeper and richer.

CHAPTER 3

Sandy

THE CAT THAT
NOBODY WANTED

Some cats lived for generations in the park, but then there were some that were dumped off because they were no longer wanted. My name is Sandy, and I'm one of the dumped cats. I am a Norwegian Forest Cat with lots of hair. I belonged to a family that fed me occasionally and allowed me to sleep in the garage. They really didn't pay much attention to me or pet me much. They wanted me to catch mice and other rodents. I was an outside cat. I roamed a bit, but I always came back. One day the family packed up and moved. I was left to fend for myself. All the important things of life were gone: meals, a warm spot to sleep, a place out of the rain, and a sense of belonging. I don't know if the family couldn't handle a cat at their new location, or if they disliked me for being a cat. Maybe they just didn't want me anymore. Like many cats before me, I have no explanation for my plight.

I roamed the neighborhood, trying to find food and a new home, but I had no success. I spotted a bird feeder at a nearby house so I stayed around there until a neighbor chased me away. Another indoor-outdoor cat lived down the street. I would visit and eat his leftover food. As time passed, I grew hungrier and thinner. One night I returned to the territory of the indoor-outdoor cat. I smelled fresh food! I noticed the food was inside a wire box, but I was too famished to care. When I walked halfway in the box, the door snapped shut. I was trapped inside a wire cage! I was petrified, but I went ahead and devoured the meal someone provided for me. It was the first decent food I'd eaten in weeks. After my tummy was full, reality kicked in. I knew if I didn't get out of that cage, I would die.

The owner of the indoor-outdoor cat came home later that evening. First, I thought he would feed me more and adopt me. Instead, I was packed up in the car and dumped in a park late at night. My new home had 500 acres of woods with many strange sounds and even stranger animals. I was used to moles, mice, squirrels, and birds, but I had never seen owls, raccoons, foxes, or deer before. I can honestly say I felt safer in a suburban or subdivision setting, and this new situation I found myself in was extremely frightening even for a big cat like me. Nobody wanted me, and I could trust no one. I tried to count my blessings. On the good side, at least I was free. The big question now was could I survive in this park?

The strange sounds and rustlings made me cower and tremble under some brush. That first night in the park was frightening, and the next night was not any better. I was so hungry by the third day I knew I needed to find food. As I roamed around, I ran into another cat named Goldie, an American Shorthair. He kept some distance between us, but he allowed me to follow him. He seemed intent on getting somewhere. After several minutes, Goldie finally stopped in some trees with lots of brush cover, near the edge of a parking lot in the park. I could see some picnic tables in the distance. It didn't make sense to just sit there and wait, but that's just what Goldie did!

Finally, a human showed up with his German Shepherd dog. Goldie walked out to the human to let him know he was there. The human had prepared Goldie some food and left it for him. I decided if I wanted something to eat, I better not be shy. I stepped out where he could see me and meowed. The human took notice and prepared a meal for me in a plastic bowl. I scarfed it down. It was my first food in more than three days. The human left, but Goldie stayed at the edge of the woods. I stayed with Goldie. A little later the human came back and fed us again. He didn't over feed us but provided the perfect amount of food. Our tummies were full. He didn't leave leftovers for the other animals to be tempted by. It was so nice to be able to eat a satisfying meal again! After eating, I investigated my new home with roads on two sides and a lake on the other sides.

As I traveled through the woods, I saw deer and raccoons foraging for food. They paid no attention to me. My heart beat a little faster when I heard the barking or yipping of foxes. At first I didn't recognize the sounds that troubled me, but I was a quick learner.

While roaming about I was always looking for something to eat. I smelled food in some trashcans, but I couldn't figure out how to get to it. I learned later from Goldie that some of the old-timers in the park had maneuvered a way to get in and out of them, which was not an easy feat. My roaming went on for several days, yielding little food. I finally returned to the portion of the park where I had originally run into Goldie. Was I ever glad to see him again! I followed Goldie again, and there was the human and his German Shepherd. I was afraid the human would not feed me. I meowed at him to get his attention and let him know I was hungry too. Goldie stared at me as if I were crazy. He knew from experience that keeping a low profile in the park was a vital key to existence. Meowing had always gotten me fed before so I knew no better!

In the days and weeks that followed, I showed up at the same place with Goldie about half of the time, meowing at the human, letting him know I was there and hungry. Sometimes the human was not there at the feeding station thirty minutes after dusk, the usual time. When he wasn't there, I would go check out the other picnic tables for food. I tried to get Goldie to follow me, but he wouldn't budge. Goldie's raspy meow encouraged me to wait, but my level of trust wasn't quite there yet.

On a couple of occasions when the human didn't show up on my timetable, I roamed to other picnic tables to find food. Sometimes I was successful, but usually not! However, when I did, I heard the human whistling in the distance for me to come to eat. I immediately headed in the direction of the whistle, meowing loudly to let the human know I was on my way. The human and

Goldie warned me to keep quiet as I traveled because my noise might invite trouble with the foxes, but meowing was the only way I got attention and food prior to living in the park so I did not see any reason to change.

One evening, while I was roaming, I heard the human's whistle and I meowed in return. This time, the foxes heard me. I had seen a fox on several other occasions; but since I was about the same size as a fox, I wasn't too concerned about a single fox attacking me. However, on this evening, the foxes came at me from at least two directions. I was cornered and in deep trouble. My only option was to scamper up a tree to escape, and that's what I did. I knew if I could wait up in the tree until dawn, then the foxes would go elsewhere. What I didn't realize was that I was cornered about sixty feet away from their den. Just when things looked hopeless, I heard the whistle of the human again. I meowed in response, but then I thought the worst. I was deep in the woods, with no way of escape. I heard the human whistle again, and he sounded closer so I meowed back. Again, the human whistled and I answered. The human was coming to me in my need. When the foxes heard the human approaching closer and caught a whiff of the German Shepherd dog that accompanied him, they scampered away. When I saw they were gone, I backed downed the tree and ran toward the human. When he spotted me, he turned around, and I followed him back to the safe place and ate a delicious meal. I was ignorant of the ways of predators in the woods. This was my first experience with life and death, but it wouldn't be my last.

On several other occasions, I was cornered by the foxes, but the human came and rescued me. Finally, I learned my lesson. I understood how important it was for me to proceed quietly through the woods when I heard the him whistle or call my name. Goldie was a stealth cat at night, and I needed to follow his example. Goldie had tried to teach me this lesson, but I had been trained by different circumstances and thought Goldie's ways were foolish. The love of the human and his provision for me made me realize that I needed to change how I lived in this hostile environment.

On another occasion, after I had learned my valuable lesson, I stumbled across some food that had been left for the foxes by the human. I didn't know how the food got there or who it was for, but I was convinced that food belonged to me. The first couple of times I discovered the foxes' food I was able to eat it without any problem. Later when I approached this food, I had encounters with raccoons and foxes. The human had his eye on me and encouraged me to leave. He called my name and his German Shepherd dog scared the animals away. I was getting wiser. I realized this was another hostile situation to be avoided. The human was feeding the foxes about 150 yards away from where he fed us cats to minimize the fight for food and survival. His love and provision taught me there was a place for all of us in the park.

The hardest time to survive in the park was in the winter months. The typical sources of food, moles, mice, and rabbits, were not very common. I really depended on the food from the human during the winter. In addition, the foxes had similar troubles in finding food and tended to be more aggressive in hunting cats or taking the cat food away. There seemed to be a delicate balance to all the wildlife in the park during the winter, and the human tried to provide for all without taking away their need to survive with their own skills.

During the summer months, I was always looking for cool spots so I tended to roam more than usual. However, my roaming had one major shortcoming in that my long fur picked up hundreds of grass burrs. Some of the grass burrs could be quite painful as they became imbedded deeper and deeper into my fur. When the human came to feed me, he petted me and realized the problem of the grass burrs. The next night while he was petting me and I was purring, he began to brush my back, sides, and tail. The result was that most of the grass burrs were removed, and I purred louder. This human was not only concerned about our eating but our total wellbeing. This human loved me unconditionally and wanted the best for me! The baggage of my upbringing was that I, Sandy, was the cat that nobody wanted. However, this human wanted me and cared for me. Better yet, I have a friend by the name of Goldie, who accepts me as I am and taught me how to survive in the park.

Life Values and Lessons from Sandy

1. Sandy felt unloved. We can relate to his pain because many of us have had similar perceptions and experiences. The damage from a painful past can take time to heal and overcome. In addition to time, we need good friends like Goldie who will accept us unconditionally for who we are and where we are. Healthy friendships, coupled with the healing and guiding hands of our Father in heaven, will keep the past from robbing us of a bright future. God never wastes our time or trials. He uses it all to accomplish His best in our lives just as He did for Sandy.

2. When we feel unwanted or unappreciated, God knows these negative behaviors and thinking must be diffused. He also knows we need others to aid in the change. God works behind the scenes, arranging events and opportunities to bring about change. Since God knows us intimately and completely, He knows what each of us needs to transform us in the image He desires for us.

3. Sandy's abandonment, loneliness, homelessness, and hunger were not wasted. Living in a hostile environment with foxes and his ignorance of life in the woods were necessary situations to make him teachable and extend friendship to Goldie. All the negative experiences became positive when Sandy's trust was restored by the only One who loved him unconditionally and accepted him. God still allows designed situations to make the unwanted of today teachable, moldable, and friendly to others and help them trust more deeply in Him.

4. Rejection and feelings of being unappreciated can paralyze us, causing us to move away from taking the proper initiatives that will enable us to move forward in a new direction, focusing our attention more on others than ourselves. Overcoming fears and hurts can be a very uncomfortable place to be, as it was for Sandy. However, in God's time, He will provide for our deepest physical, emotional, mental, and spiritual needs with unique opportunities, loyal friendships, and a sense of His power and presence for our best. His provision is always sufficient, whether for daily needs or for protection from multi-directional attacks. He wants us to enjoy our lives, and we will if we trust Him and seek to please Him.

5. One of the key factors to remember as we walk through any negative emotion is this: God knows our name and is fully aware of our past, present, and future. Not only does He know our name and the number of hairs on our head, but He is fully aware of our strengths and our weaknesses. He looks at us through the eyes of love, and if we allow Him to, He will make the best version of us possible. He sees our potential for good and our tendency for bad. Yet He loves us unconditionally and accepts us right where we are. He knows what we could become with His miraculous touch of grace. Through His love and help, feelings of rejection and being unappreciated will disappear just as the morning fog on a lake disappears with the rising sun. May we rest in His knowledge of us and trust Him to complete His unique work in us!

CHAPTER 4

Park

THE CAT THAT
WAS MISTREATED

As an adult gray and white tabby, there was so much of my kittenhood I didn't remember. There were flashes of recollections, but none were pleasant! Once when I was a kitten, I was held captive in a cage outside under a tree with no protection from the weather. When it rained, I got drenched! The thunder and lightning frightened me, but I was trapped. There was no place to run so I curled up in the corner of my small cage. Some days I didn't have any food to eat. I would scrounge around and frequently ate leftovers from someone's table. There were times I wouldn't have gotten a bite to eat if I hadn't cried a lot, hoping to be noticed and fed. My begging for food was frequently met with brutal and cutting words, along with someone beating on my cage with a huge stick. As frightened as I was, I knew I had to get something to eat. I had lost quite a bit of weight and my ribs were showing. I was underweight, about half of what a kitten my age should weigh.

I did have water unless I turned over the water bowl, and then I would have to wait for the next feeding before my water bowl was refilled. I was never taken out of the cage except for an occasional cleaning. I was never picked up, petted, hugged, or loved on and I had no name except Cat. My life was a miserable existence, but I had nothing to compare with. I figured it was normal to be mistreated and abused. The fact I didn't purr didn't faze me, because I didn't know any different!

I was growing weaker and weaker and realized my chance of survival was pretty bleak if my circumstances didn't change. What should have been the most joyous and fun time of my life ended up being the worst. When I reached the deepest depths of despair, the small cage I was trapped in was picked up and I was placed in the trunk of a car. I had seen cars before, but I had never been inside one. Thirty minutes later, I found myself at a park with picnic tables. They dumped me off with a little food and no water. I had very mixed emotions. I was excited to be free from the cage but fearful of my new surroundings. I scurried to the edge of the woods. My body trembled as I studied my new home.

That first day I didn't travel very far from the edge of the woods, and I didn't sleep well that night. The park was filled with lots of strange noises. Car engines roaring past the picnic table and the constant yipping of foxes kept me awake. Hunger pangs drove me out of hiding in search of food scraps the next day. I found a little food and also discovered there was a lake about forty yards through the woods. I was relieved I wasn't in an abusive environment anymore, but I wasn't sure I could survive in the wild because I hadn't had the privilege of being trained by my parents how to hunt small game. I had gone from one bad situation to another, which could be deadly since the yipping of the foxes was growing closer every night. My circumstances looked bleak again!

Just when I thought I may not make it, a human showed up at the picnic table. He sang songs and whistled. When I stuck my head out of the woods, he spotted me immediately. He coaxed me out of the woods with soft words of praise and some food. He didn't try to touch me but calmed my anxious heart with his soothing tones. Wow! These were the first encouraging words I had ever heard. Plus the good food was a bonus. When he left, I ran back to my cover in the woods, hoping he would come again. The next day he was back with more food and canned milk. I had not tasted milk since the early days of my life. I was so excited seeing the food, milk, and this human that I let him pet me. As he stroked me and talked, I purred, something I had never done in all the days of my mistreatment.

I looked forward to the visits with the human in the evening. There was always enough food, milk, and lots of petting. He even picked me up and remarked about how thin I was and was concerned because I was very undernourished. He warned me about the foxes and told me how they had cornered other cats and killed them. The human was genuinely concerned for me! I could tell! When he left, though, I retreated to the edge of the woods. I cringed when I heard the foxes yipping at night.

One night the foxes' yipping sounded unusually close. As I peered out from my hiding place, I saw one of them sniffing around the picnic table. I knew he was either looking for food or he was out to get me. The next day the human came in the morning and in the evening. His visit in the morning was not his typical visit. After he fed me, he searched the grass and dirt around the table. He sat down with me after a few minutes and commented it was time to do something. The threat from the foxes was getting too great, and I was not a woods-smart cat so my chances for survival were slim. When he held me and promised to return that evening, I purred. True to his word, he appeared with a strange container that he sat in the grass. After he fed me, he picked me up and talked about finding me a new home where I could be loved and cared for. He was adamant about protecting me from the foxes. He placed me in the container and put me in his vehicle. This was the second car ride of my life. I was scared and meowing, but the human took me to a house where there were several other cats. They roamed freely on this property with an easy entrance and exit to the house. However, I was placed in a bathroom with plenty of food, milk, and love. Several times a day the human would come and sit with me and stroke my thick fur. Since I had spent all my kitten life in a cage, I was afraid I may be stuck for the rest of my life trapped in this bathroom.

Other people would visit me in the bathroom. They even gave me a new name—Park. I liked it. They fed me and held me. A few days later, I was placed in a cage and taken to a vet for a medical checkup and neutering. All the people at the vet's office remarked how beautiful I was, even with my bony ribs poking out. The vet assured me I had found a new home. When we arrived back at the house, the human placed me back in the bathroom, but several times a day he would put a small leash on me and take me outside. I knew he wanted me to get accustomed to my new home. He told me there were foxes around there, but the local dogs frightened most of them off. I ran and hid in the tall grass, but the human would rein me in. It was great to be able to run without fear of being mistreated for going too far. These trips outside lasted for a couple of weeks, and during them I was introduced to some other cats: Asa, Cassidy, and Leo. Asa and Cassidy seemed to tolerate me, but the rescued and adopted cat named Leo allowed me rub against him and sit with him, all the while on the leash. I was also introduced to a big German Shepherd dog named Wiggles. She watched over all the cats and the property.

I really didn't enjoy being returned and stuck in the bathroom. In my mind, the room was just a larger cage. My anxieties were always relieved when the human fed me, loved on me, and talked to me. But one afternoon, I had the surprise of my life. The human opened up the bathroom door and gave me full run of the house. He still penned me up in the bathroom at night, but I think he did that because he knew I felt safer that way. He explained to me later that I needed time to get stronger to take care of myself and to become familiar with the surroundings so I could call it home.

On one of my curiosity searches through the house, I found a small door at the bottom of a larger door the other cats entered and exited through. They came in, ate, and found the human for some affection. Once they were satisfied, they would leave through the small door. After observing this coming and going through this cat door for a couple days, I followed Leo out this same door. My breath was taken away by what I found. Outdoors with my new friend, Leo, there were large trees, high grass, lots of woods, a big dry creek bed, and lots of places to roam. I thought I had died and gone to cat heaven. I tagged along with Leo outside all day long. It was great! I watched him hunt squirrels and mice. Later, I found out from the other cats that Leo had lived in the wild for years just existing off the animals he killed for food. Leo was considered the toughest of the cats and the best hunter. What a privilege and honor to be taught by the best!

To show the human I appreciated the compassion he had showered upon me, I carried my first squirrel and dropped it at his feet. This was the first of many gifts I would bring the human. He smiled when he saw me coming at different times with various gifts: a can, a piece of bark, a pinecone, a piece of cloth, and even a live bird.

As a kitten, I had endured terrible abuse, but the acceptance and love of my new home made all the pain of my past worthwhile. The human protected, provided food and shelter, and loved me unconditionally. I am one grateful cat!

One day after living in my new home for several months, the human sat with me in the grass scratching my ears, my chin, my tummy, and my back. He spoke my love language. My emotional tank was filled up because of these special times. While sitting there enjoying his presence, the human told me he had observed some unique things about me. He had noticed how well I got along with all the cats. He called me the peacemaker in the family. Maybe it was the mistreatment and traumatic kittenhood that made me adaptable and friendly to other cats. Whatever it was, the human wanted me to use my leadership skills to help other cats adapt to their new home.

There was another feral cat named Tiny, who had lost his parents at a very young age. He was foraging on his own in the big park. On several occasions the foxes tracked Tiny with the intent of making a meal out of him. The human brought Tiny home and wanted me to help him. He was a beautiful black and white tuxedo tabby. Even though he was all muscle and looked strong, he was very scared of his new surroundings. Tiny and the human were very close. After the new cat was comforted by the human, Tiny and I ran around together playing and investigating all of the woods and surrounding fields. Even Leo, the older cat who had taken me under his wing, went with us. It was great having friends to romp and play with! It was great having a master to purr for!

Life Values and Lessons from Park

1. All of us have been mistreated in some way and at some time in our lives. Some of us have endured horrific abuse that has been so cruel and continuous that we frequently felt the problem was with us and not with the abusers. Victims are robbed of hope, value, and dignity, twisting their perceptions of what is normal, as Park did. The Father in heaven sees it all and intervenes at "the right moment." The divine intervention may be a complete or partial rescue from the situation or may be a movement to another hopeless and helpless situation from which God can engineer a unique solution that brings Him greater glory and honor.

2. When an individual has been mistreated like Park, there are invisible cages built around their freedoms, expression, perceptions,

thinking, and every area of their lives. Over time, the Father's gentle hand can release them from these bondages. Many times He works through others who view them as God does, offering hope and healing to seemingly hopeless situations. May we see God working and respond properly!

3. All the mistreatment and abuse Park endured or we have endured, God can use for good. He will never waste our hurtful experiences or time. Difficulties can change us as they did Park! He became a better cat and displayed his love and appreciation for the human with the gifts he gave to him. His peacemaking abilities, his gentle love and acceptance of others, and his freedom to be who God had ordained him to be also show the tremendous change taking place in his life. Likewise, God will use all that has happened in our life—the good, the bad, and the very worst—to help us love Him more deeply, to love ourselves for who we are, and to love and serve others.

4. May we give praise to our Father in heaven, who not only sees our mistreatment but who also recognizes our great value and gave His only Son to die for us! He provides words of encouragement and empowerment from others and from His Word. Listen attentively!

5. Some reading this story will immediately identify with the lack of hope, value, purpose, and dignity Park endured because of the mistreatment or abuse they have suffered in their own lives. Others may experience such mistreatment at a later time, so don't forget that God sees and intervenes. However, God may ask you to provide grace, love, and aid to someone who has been mistreated or abused. There are no quick fixes for such aid and comfort to another. But be sure the reward in heaven is great for gifts of love, time, and ourselves we give to restore or to provide healing for those who cross our paths who have been or are being mistreated or abused. Cats cannot hide their abuse very well, but people can. We need to pray for eyes to see their pain, their bondages from the past, and their great potential for the future. Such divine discernment in tandem with love will yield thirty, sixty, or hundredfold in fruit for the kingdom of God.

CHAPTER 5

Tiny

THE CAT THAT
WAS A MISTAKE

Of all of the cats that lived or were born in the park, my story is one of the most unusual because of my unique beginning and journey. My name is Tiny. I never knew my father, but here are the facts I learned from the human during our many late night conversations. My father was a very large black and white tuxedo tabby. He weighed about seventeen pounds and was an indoor cat that lived in a house on the edge of the park property. When you went by the house, you would see my father sitting in the window, anxious to get outside. Sometime later, he did get out and disappeared for several weeks. The human found my father hunting in some marshland about a mile away. The human informed the owner of the whereabouts of my father, and the owner retrieved his cat. That should have been the end of my story, but instead it was just the beginning!

While I never knew my father, I have vague memories of my mother. I was on my own at a very young age. It was very difficult to learn the art of survival without proper training from your father and mother. At six months, I discovered some food lying by the park road every evening. There was a smorgasbord of different foods: wieners, chicken, and dog food. Later I learned this was a fox feeding station, and the human knew I didn't have a chance against the foxes so he did his best to keep me as far from them as he could. The human noticed my small frame and named me Tiny. Occasionally, the human spotted me moving through the tall grass and weeds, hunting and hopping like a rabbit. I had no fear of anything, but the human was concerned I did not seem to have the woods' smarts to survive. I was always on the hunt for more food.

One night I heard a whistle and went to investigate. The human was leaving some food for another cat named Blackie, who had lived in the park for several years. He saw me from a distance, spoke my name, and left another small pile of dry cat food under the picnic table. It was the first time I did not have to scrounge for food. Most days I would have to hide in the woods downwind from the foxes and eat the leftovers, which were few. If I could get to the fox food before the foxes, then I would have a good meal, but I was always running for cover at the slightest sound. One night the foxes showed up and chased me up a tree. While I was stranded in the tree, I realized I needed to find a regular source of food. The next night I went back to the picnic table where Blackie was fed. The human showed up again and left food for Blackie and me. He stepped back from the table and talked to me while I finished eating. I was so hungry I gobbled my food without too much chewing.

Every evening I would show up at the table and the human would feed me. One evening I was starving and I let the human pet me while I devoured my meal. I was eating, purring, and being petted all at the same time. On another occasion the human brought me a small container of milk. Wow! That was the first milk I had tasted since I nursed from my mother a few months before when I was only six months old. I enjoyed drinking that milk! I liked the routine I found myself in. I was at the picnic table and the human always fed Blackie and me. I trusted the human more and more. He picked me up for short periods of time and petted me while I purred. Rain or shine, the human was faithful to come and feed us.

The den of the foxes was less than eighty yards away from the picnic table where I often ate. I heard the foxes yipping at night, and sometimes their crying seemed closer than usual. The human saw the foxes hunting and began feeding me twice at night! At first, I didn't understand why, but after I thought about it, I was confident he was making sure I finished all the food he provided, leaving no scraps to attract the foxes. I also thought he was making sure I was safe when he fed me a second time. There were a few occasions when the foxes showed up at the table, sniffing around for food. It was mid-winter and food was scarce in the park, especially since we had just experienced a drought. I knew my situation was not safe, but I needed to eat so I had to take a chance.

On one unusually cold windy night, I was upwind from the foxes. After being fed by the human, I heard the foxes coming closer. Two of them approached me from different directions. My options for escape were limited! Just when my heart skipped a beat, the human showed up, and the foxes hurried away. The human knew I was no match for the foxes. He picked me up and placed me in a small cage. My heart stopped racing after he rescued me, but now my life in the park seemed over. What was next?

I went on a short drive with the human. He brought me to a house with lots of trees, grass, and room to roam, but then he placed me in a small bathroom. For about a week, I was well fed and loved on. The human was happy because I purred a lot. He and I both knew if he hadn't rescued me from the foxes, I would have died.

Life in the bathroom was very interesting. I met another cat named Park. He poked his paws under the door and played with me. Other cats sniffed at the door, but then they walked on by. After a week of solitary confinement, the human let me out of the bathroom. The setting was so strange in a house, and it scared me since I was used to living in the woods. I saw Park and the other cats exit through a cat door. I followed, not knowing where the adventure would lead.

Immediately, I was outside in the woods with plenty of places to hide. While the woods were similar to what I was familiar with, they were different.

I enjoyed my freedom again. My new friend, Park, introduced me to Leo, a gorgeous orange mackerel cat. Leo would tolerate me, and the three of us would roam in the woods and play. At night, all the cats went into the house to eat and sleep, but I stayed outside. The human came out and whistled for me as he did in the park and fed me outside. He continued this routine for several weeks. Being a very observant cat, I noticed the cats always came out in the morning and returned in the evening. During the day, as the human would come and go, he would leave small piles of food outside. He whistled and all of us cats came running. The reward was special food!

One night we had a horrible rainstorm with lots of lightning. I was drenched and scared. Timidly, I went into the house. The human was waiting for me and dried me off with a towel. He did this for all the other cats too. He soothed my fears when he loved on me and fed me. That night I understood for the first time what the other cats already knew. The human's house was a safe haven from the weather and other predators. I had a nice warm and dry place to sleep that night, and even Park snuggled up close to me and kept me company.

As the weeks past, I followed the human around everywhere. Every time he loved on me, I would purr. I was still very skittish when I heard unusual sounds, but now that I had a home and friends, I had no fear. Most important of all, I was close to the human, and he loved me no matter what my past was and was extremely patient with me in adjusting to a new life. Life couldn't get any better. I was one blessed cat!

Life Values and Lessons from Tiny

1. Tiny had no control of the mistakes made by his parents. He could not be faulted for his upbringing. Such mistakes can have far-reaching consequences on attitudes, perspectives of others, and the future. These were things Tiny could not control. What is obvious from Tiny's story is that God will turn the stumbling blocks of our past hurts into stepping-stones to bring healing into our lives. God can use mistakes, jaded backgrounds, and poor upbringing to accomplish much good in the life of the

individual and in the life of others if we will allow Him to have His perfect and sovereign way with us. If we rest in His unique sovereignty for each of us, the result will be much glory and praise for our Father in heaven.

2. Even in Tiny's youth, ignorance, and lack of training in surviving in the world, God provided for him and protected him. God feeds the birds of the air. Will He not care for a cat? Will he not help people with baggage from their past? God's provision is sometimes not seen as coming from His hand, but it always does. His protection is frequently not understood nor appreciated, but it ultimately is extremely great. May our God open our eyes to see all He does in providing for and protecting us.

3. Tiny had to make many adjustments in living and surviving. These were difficult adjustments! The times were dark and very draining, but God is always there even in those tough adjustments or trying times. Not only is God ever present and ever knowledgeable about our tough circumstances, but He is also very patient and loving toward us while going through these situations. God will even use these times to mold us into the kind of people He can use in ministering to others who come across our path.

4. Mistakes in our past, learning from those errors, and making tough adjustments in line with God's best for us now can be difficult. However, friends like Park and Leo who have gone through similar difficulties can be a tremendous encouragement and help in making the adjustments and learning from them. May our arms be full with friends who love us unconditionally!

CHAPTER 6

Leo

THE CAT THAT
HAD A HARD LIFE

My origins are not in the park. I grew up about a mile away along some creek bottoms and woods. I am an orange mackerel cat with the markings of a snow leopard. That's why the human named me Leo. I was another disposable cat left in the neighborhood when his owners moved. I had always hunted rabbits, mice, squirrels, and other small rodents (but not birds). I am a very social cat that craved people contact, but almost everyone I wanted to befriend chased me off. None of the neighborhood cats had anything to do with me either. I went days without eating, which explained my thinness and unsightly looks. I met another orange cat on my wanderings named Cassidy and followed him to his home. Some days there was dry cat food left outside so I finished the leftovers. There were numerous walnut trees in this neck of the woods with plenty of squirrels so I decided to stay in the area.

However, something happened to me. I had difficulty eating and keeping food down. I was losing weight and getting very thin. One day the human coaxed me to come to him. I would have been happy for the little attention he was giving me, but then he fed and loved on me. This was the first affection I had experienced in years. For several days he showered me with loving kindness in an attempt to build my trust in him. He noticed how skinny I was and the difficulty I had eating. The human told me I would not live much longer without medical attention. The next thing I knew he picked me up, placed me in a cat carrier, and took me to the veterinarian.

The veterinarian checked my mouth and discovered my problem, I had a major abscess in my gums and teeth. He told the human I would die if I did not have an operation immediately. The poison in the abscessed tooth had spread throughout my body and weakened me. The vet quickly informed the human I needed to have the bad tooth removed and my gums repaired. Time was short and survival was risky in my weakened state, but the human loved me. He had compassion on me because he knew I had lived a difficult life. The human told the vet to go ahead with the surgery because he appreciated my attitude and sweet spirit despite all the sorrows I had experienced. He provided a way for me to have a second chance at life. My surgery was successful. Immediately the toxins were leaving my body. A few days after surgery I was able to eat normally again, but even better than regaining my physical health was the fact I had found a forever home with an eternal friend!

I made two new cat friends at my new home—Cassidy and Asa. They were complete opposites in their personalities. Asa had nothing to do with me, but Cassidy tolerated me. This relationship tiff did not bother me since the human loved me unconditionally. His love allowed me to define my place or role among the other cats.

The first role I took on was protector. Several roaming tomcats came into our newly adopted territory. I fought and defended my new home with all my strength. Those tomcats seldom came back, but when they did, I declared war on them. Sometimes I was dinged up with missing hair and flesh wounds. The human stopped by the vet's office and bought some medicine for me. On a couple of occasions, I tangled with raccoons. The human shook his head and told me I just didn't know when to back down and leave well enough alone. All the other cats ran for cover when the tomcats or raccoons appeared on the scene, but not me. I would fight! In several of those scuffles, I was so hurt that the human ran me back to the vet again to get stitched up. I always recovered, and the vet and I became good friends. One of the reasons for the fights was the fact I didn't want to come inside unless it was very cold. I had lived outside in the elements all my life, and I wasn't going to change. I was an outdoorsy kind of cat and usually ended up sleeping in the garage.

I continued to have more infections in my mouth so there were more trips back to the vet. I wasn't able to eat because my mouth was so sore and inflamed. The human monitored my condition and the types of food he fed me, but I still got sick. Of all the cats, I became the best at taking medicine. I had a lot of practice!

My second role was mentoring the new rescued cats. When Park, a mistreated cat, was brought into the human's home, I was his immediate friend. I taught him some very important lessons: how to hunt, how to avoid aggressive dogs, and how to stay within the boundaries of our range. When Tiny, the cat that was a mistake, was rescued, I taught him how to socialize with the other cats and to move quietly through the neighborhood unseen. Whenever it rained, the human knew he'd find Park, Tiny, and me outside. All of us had been conditioned by our environment and were able to brave the elements. The human continually dried off three sopping wet cats after the rainstorms. I was considerably older than Park and Tiny. They considered me the closest thing to a father figure they'd ever had. I enjoyed my role in my new home, but I enjoyed sitting on the human's lap and being loved on even more. I never knew what love was like until this human looked beyond my unsightliness, my pains and struggles, and my loneliness. He saw my potential and gave me the chance to be loved and to love.

Life Values and Lessons from Leo

1. Leo had experienced rejection and craved affection. He was
    forced to survive on his own any way he could, leaving him
    with many physical and emotional scars. He was acquainted
    with sickness and felt unadoptable, but love changed
    everything. When he finally found a home, experienced love,
    and contributed to the needs of others, he began to sense
    his worth. As adults and children, we all go through similar
    experiences. Some have gone through dire circumstances most
    of their lives. We can be confident that God sees it all and is
    working behind the scenes to use every trial to mold us and
    prepare us for great things. As we yield to God and let Him
    have His way, we discover peace and comfort in the adventure
    and a unique plan that He has for each of us. God led Leo to
    what he could never have had by his own effort. God's ways
    are mysterious but ever purposeful for us and others.

2. Leo's difficult times uniquely prepared him for his role as
    protector and mentor. Likewise, not only the hard times, but
    also the good times, will be used by God to prepare us for
    the role of serving Him and others. Our joys and sorrows are
    sovereignly ordered and timed to accomplish God's best for
    us. When we are passing through these experiences, it may
    be extremely difficult to see God's hand and purpose; but we
    need to give thanks to Him and keep trusting in Him alone. It
    looked like a chaos of pain and difficulties for Leo, but in the
    end there were love and peace.

3. Because of Leo's hardships, he had a unique set of gifts and
    abilities that enabled him to survive in the wild. The difficulties
    he faced honed his survival skills, something the younger or
    less mature cats needed to know. Leo blossomed in the new
    place God planted him in as he shared what he knew with a
    younger generation. We too need to blossom where God has
    planted us and continually strive to invest in others.

4. No matter how lonely we are or how many hurts, sicknesses, or wounds we experience, God always sees potential in each of us. We can be all He wants us to be when we tap into the grace and power of God. We need to understand God never wastes our pain. He comforts us so we can encourage others with the same encouragement He has given to us. God receives all the glory instead of us. After all, He is the Author of it all!

CHAPTER 7

Cord

THE CAT THAT
WAS BULLIED

My name is Cord and my origins are not in the park. I was another of those "disposable" cats someone dumped off. When the human met me, he told me someone missed a tremendous blessing by not knowing me. I could have been abandoned because I was not one of those beautiful cats or maybe my former owners had health issues. I never knew the real reason, but many times I thought about why they just dropped me off and left me. They could have faced economic difficulties, forcing them to move and leave me behind. I learned from the human that the way my life started doesn't determine who I am. He told me many cats have had challenging beginnings but lived their lives with purpose and direction. I guess it doesn't make any difference why I was dumped because my story doesn't really begin until my appearance in the park. I showed up around the time the drought was in its first year and the foxes were hunting anything that was small with four legs. The park was protected on three sides by water and a bridge that kept out the cat's worst predator, the coyote.

Somehow, I found my way to a county maintenance shop in the park, where I was fed by some of the workers. I met some other cats living there and we got along really well. The foxes didn't bother the cats living at the maintenance facility because of all the people, machines, and activity going on. The maintenance shop was a safe zone from predators, and we cats were generally fed twice a day. Even the rodents stayed close to the shop in the drought, which provided the cats with another source of food. It was a comfortable existence, but there was not much love given to a big muscular cat like me. I developed some friendships there with Little Bit, Midnight, and Blue. However, after a year a new male cat by the name of TJ showed up. TJ was born in the park. In fact, his mother was one of the cats at the maintenance shop, but she continually moved her kittens around to avoid detection from the foxes and people. When TJ showed up, he was aggressive and immediately claimed the shop as his territory. The first thing he did was start picking on the cat he didn't like, and guess who that was. Me! As to seniority, I had first rights. However, that didn't mean much in the cat world. At first TJ just hissed at me, but then his violence escalated to tougher encounters at feeding time that left fur flying. TJ chased me whenever he saw me. I was a big cat, but I could outrun most other cats. Because I was swifter, I usually escaped or climbed the nearest tree. On a few occasions, TJ stalked me in an attempt to do harm, but I wasn't intimidated by his bullying. I had learned how to avoid the foxes and used the same techniques on TJ. I knew I needed to move on, but I had no idea where!

Since I had good wood-smarts, I investigated other options at night. On one of my excursions, I came across the human feeding Sandy, a cat I had never seen before, and, Goldie, a cat I had seen occasionally at the maintenance shop. I was hungry so I marched up to them, trying to get a bite to eat, but the human wouldn't let me feed at the same location. Instead, he fed me over by a trashcan. He used his German Shepherd dog to herd me to the right spot so I would not tangle with Sandy. I quickly learned if I waited around the parking lot, the human would feed me near the trashcan every evening. It was the first regular food I had eaten in months!

I was a little pushy, wanting to eat at the same place as Sandy and Goldie. Sandy was opposed to my sharing a meal with them, but Goldie had no problem with it. Sometimes Sandy would chase me up a tree when I got too close to his territory. Over time, I realized that being fed next to the trashcan had its strategic advantages. I could see down the hill on one side and across the flat parking lot on the other from that point of view. In addition, I could run to some large cedar trees that were real close if there was trouble. Sandy tried to bully me some, but the human used the German Shepherd dog to herd and keep Sandy in his place as well. After a while everyone knew their place, and harmony existed. I began allowing the human to stroke my fur every day more and more. It was the highlight of my day and I purred every time he stroked me.

I enjoyed my life as a cat. What more could I ask for? I had freedom, food, love from the human, and protection. He wouldn't allow any bullying. Life was on an upswing. That is until TJ the bully showed up. He attacked and chased off Sandy and me. In fact, Sandy ran almost a mile away in one direction while I ran about a mile in the opposite direction. For some reason, TJ did not pick on Goldie. I couldn't understand why. Then I figured it was because Goldie held his ground, and the human fed Goldie, but not TJ, because TJ's food was at the maintenance shop. The human kept using the German Shepherd dog to keep TJ in his place.

The human searched for almost a week before he located Sandy and me. Once he found us, he fed us and then whistled at night so we would return to our normal feeding area. The human was determined to help Sandy and me work through the issues with TJ's bullying. TJ had the cruel habit of sneaking up behind Sandy and me and attacking us. Then he would finish eating our food. As the human realized what TJ was doing, he relied on Sandy's and my keen sense of smell and hearing to move the German Shepherd into position to spoil the attacks. Sometimes TJ would chase Sandy and me up different trees, but the human refused to feed TJ. Finally I realized I needed to sit in the middle of the parking lot so TJ could not get to me without being seen. Sandy did the same thing on the edge of the tree line. This strategy helped most of the time, but I felt rushed when I ate.

Since this conflict was always at night, the human started coming early in the morning to feed me and the rest of the cats to avoid TJ's bullying. The human's wisdom helped keep me in the same area as Sandy and Goldie.

Nighttime in this section of the park was always tense so the human decided to try to feed TJ at a different spot. He used the German Shepherd to herd TJ to where he wanted him to go. He stood guard with his German Shepherd so the other cats and I could eat without being bullied. The human also removed any uneaten food from the other feeding spots. Whenever the guard wasn't set, TJ continued to bully the other cats. However, the stress was greatly reduced! Whenever I felt it wasn't safe with TJ around or that Sandy might pick on me, I followed the human and the German Shepherd around on their walk of a couple of miles. I always felt safe in the sight of the human or in his presence. Sometimes the human unfolded a chair and sat in the parking lot. I loved those moments when I jumped in the human's lap and he showered me with love and attention. I was thrilled I had found someone to help me deal with my bully TJ.

TJ's bullying made the other cats tense too as evidenced by Sandy chasing me some. The human decided he needed to move my feeding station to a more open area close to the water and near a big cedar tree. This new feeding spot allowed me to see if TJ or other cats were coming. I also climbed the cedar tree to get away from TJ or Sandy, but better yet, I climbed the tree and used it as a lookout for other cats. This new feeding spot allowed me more one-on-one time with the human. Without the human's help, my life would have been miserable. Now I could relax and let down my guard. I enjoyed being a friendly cat! My beginnings may have been a little rough, but this cat life seems to have a "purr"fect ending!

Life Values and Lessons from Cord

1. There will always be bullies! Most of the time we think only children or adolescents experience bullies on playgrounds or at school. Some surveys indicate that almost one out of every two children and adolescents are bullied during their school years. This bullying can be either verbal or physical, but the

consequences of such bullying can leave emotional scars, not to mention the damage it does to the victims socially, physically, and even mentally. However, bullies exist for adults as well— intellectual bullies, cyberspace bullies, envy bullies, and more. Cord's first strategy in dealing with the bully TJ was avoiding or just keeping a healthy distance between himself and the bully. That strategy worked for a while, but TJ wanted to be first in all or to have his way at the maintenance shop. Cord was seen as a threat to it all so TJ bullied him. Cord's second strategy in dealing with the bully was the exit strategy, which is going somewhere else since no one was helping Cord deal with the bully. That strategy had a short-lived benefit too.

2. Cord needed food, love, and total acceptance, as well as someone to help him work through the bullying. At the right time, God will provide someone to aid the victim of bullying. The human had to teach Cord how to avoid and deal with bullying in his new location. He trained Cord to recognize the situations and always be wary of bullies. He provided Cord with some space and exit strategies. After all Cord learned to do, he knew he may have to fight as a last resort. However, just as the human began feeding Cord in the morning to build his confidence and to build his trust in the human, God will also provide a safe haven to repair the damage the bully has done and to build the trust in Him the victim must have to win over fear.

3. God used the human and his dog to keep TJ and Sandy in their proper place and to bring an end to the bullying. TJ had to learn the hard way that his behavior of controlling or dominating other cats was not acceptable. God's strategy of divine intervention by people was key to ending the bullying cycle. The nation of Israel was bullied by Goliath the Philistine and his descendants, and God used David the shepherd and his soldiers to deal with this family of bullies. God still uses others to help in the battle with bullies!

4. Sometimes parents, teachers, and those in authority do not understand the consequences and hardships that bullying brings on the victims. They think the bullying will pass without any long-term effects. However, if these young bullies continue into adulthood, it is not a phase that will pass. Instead, it will become worse! We need to see this bullying as God sees it, a

stench. It destroys not only the one bullied but also the bully himself. Victims of the bullying mindsets are warped. They begin thinking there is something wrong with them when the problem is really with the bully. This thinking can lead to some disastrous results for the victims. But victims of bullying, like Cord, need to be encouraged that God sees it all. God will use the challenges to make the victim beautiful in His sight as we trust in Him just as Cord trusted in the human to help him deal with his bullies.

CHAPTER 8

Callie

THE CAT THAT WAS A
MOTHER OF EXCELLENCE

My mother and father lived in a colony of feral cats located in an old marble quarry that was no longer in operation. This quarry was surrounded by water on three sides and a road on the other. It was less than two miles from the main park but across the road from fishing piers, trash barrels, and more water. The quarry was a protected environment, but food sources were scarce, especially during the winter months. Because of this, my parents would spend quite a bit of time across the road searching for food during the cold weather conditions.

My name is Callie. According to the human's description of me, I am a beautiful calico cat. I lived in the quarry. My parents and I had many ways to get to the other side of the road: by way of a drainage pipe (which was the safest but not always passable), under a bridge (the longest way), or by running across the road to the fishing piers (the shortest but not the safest route). The food options were fish, trash leftovers, and occasional dry cat food. For a year or two, someone left a bag of cat food in the woods near the piers. While this feeding was not done regularly, it sure helped keep us from starving, but when it rained the food was a soggy mess and not edible! Eventually, the human took over my feeding. The pier area was very open with some trees and brush along the lake. The first difficulty he had was finding a safe place to feed me away from people and out of the wind and rain and especially the snow during the winter. He finally discovered a rock overhang and constructed a small brush lean-to to hide the entrance.

I was a very gentle cat and roamed about a half mile in all directions every evening looking for food scraps and dead fish. Since I was such a loner, a glimpse of me was very rare. Even when the human fed me, I would not let him get very close to me. I was a woods savvy cat and knew about raccoons, foxes, people, dogs, and coyotes. I slipped through the woods without making a sound. The human fed me every night for about six months, and all of sudden I disappeared for a couple of weeks. He thought something bad had happened to me, but his fears were relieved when I reappeared. I was very hungry and gobbled down two big helpings of food. I became friendlier but still kept my distance. Because of my calico coloring, I could sit camouflaged among the brush in the woods. Hardly anyone knew I was there unless I moved or they were looking for me.

One evening about eight weeks after my disappearance, I showed up with my three kittens: Rub, Copper, and Grey. Those little ones were my reason for disappearing. All of us were hungry, but the human had plenty of food as well as canned milk mixed with water. The kittens scrambled for food while I just went for the milk. This went on for months and finally the father of my kittens, a longhaired yellow tabby, showed up. He kept his distance and only ate after the rest had eaten. He had lots of scars on his face so the human could tell he was a very tough cat, but there was an air of majesty about him as well. My mate, Scar, made himself visible to the human about once a month, but the kittens and I were there every night. My family was beautiful, but the human pointed out to me that I was the glue that held it together!

Sometimes the human came early in the morning to feed the kittens and me. One of the early cold spring mornings, I was sitting at the front of one of my dens in the quarry where I could look for the human. This particular den was about 100 yards away from the feeding station at the fishing piers. The human arrived and whistled for me and walked around looking for me since I always showed up close to feeding time. His whistle could be heard a long way off, and whenever I heard it, I hightailed to wherever he was. He called my name and finally spotted me on a rock formation outside my den, but across a busy road from the fishing piers. I think he just wanted to make sure I was safe. Was he in for a surprise! I know he was not expecting what happened next. I woke up the kittens, and they followed me to the edge of the dangerous road. I looked both ways and listened intently as I had been taught by my parents. And then I moved across the road with my kittens behind me. If there had been more traffic, we would have gone around a longer safer way, but nursing kittens takes a lot of energy and nourishment. A few weeks after the road crossing, my kitten Grey did not return. The human thought he may have been hit by a car, but I think a coyote may have gotten him. After Grey disappeared, we moved from that den and I kept my kittens closer to me. I warmed up to the human. Rub and I trotted out to the human's car to be petted, and Rub would continually rub against the human's leg. Copper was shy and stayed back at the edge of the woods.

When Rub and Copper were almost a year old, the human informed me my kittens and I needed to be neutered. He didn't want the cat colony to grow any bigger because the pier environment could not sustain our lives if the human didn't show up and take care of us. After losing Grey, he wanted to help prevent any more tragedies. The human first trapped Rub and got him neutered and then released him again, but he had trouble trapping Copper and me. I was very suspicious. I sniffed at all of the different traps and kept my distance. The human told me I was one of the smartest cats he had ever known! A short time later, I didn't show up for several weeks. Rub and Copper went without me. When they returned home, they told me the human was asking about me and was very concerned. I was pregnant again, and this pregnancy seemed different. I hunted close to the den to save energy. Four weeks later, I showed up with Rub and Copper, but I was moving slower than usual.

I was still a loving mother to Rub and Copper, but I had gained a lot more weight during this pregnancy compared to my last. The human was very concerned about how large I was and my overall health. He checked on me in the mornings. One particular Saturday morning when the human checked on me, he found a stillborn kitten. He knew I was in trouble and took a large fishing net, crawled into the woods on his hands and knees, and captured me with the fishing net. I didn't like it one bit. I was in great pain and shock! The human hurried me to the veterinarian. On the way there, he said something to me about hoping to save me and my kittens, but if the vet couldn't save my kittens, he hoped the vet could at least save me. I delivered another kitten and named him Rust. The vet believed I could deliver the rest of the kittens naturally. After giving me some fluids, he sent me and my kitten home with the human. Once we got home and settled in, I grew weaker and wasn't very responsive I tried to lick my newborn kitten as he tried to nurse, but I felt lightheaded. The human knew something was wrong. He was right. I had gone into shock and couldn't care for Rust. Before we could get Rust back to the vet, he died. The human rushed me back to the vet and a cesarean was performed. I had a dead kitten in my womb. The surviving kitten was a female gray tabby with brown splotches. I named her Grace! After several more trips to the vet, I grew stronger and started responding to little Grace. It was a hard battle for life for mother and kitten, but we made it together!

Grace and I lived in the human's bathroom for several months until I got my strength back. Every time the human checked on us, he petted me and picked up Grace. At first, I would bristle and worry, but eventually I grew to trust the human and realized he meant no harm to Grace. Occasionally, the human packed us up. Then he took Grace and me back to the pier so Rub and Copper knew we were all right. Rub always sniffed the carrier, but he was more interested in eating than reconnecting with his mother. This happened several times. The human said he needed to do this because he hoped to release us back to our original environment. However, in the transition time of trying to return me back to the colony I held together, raccoons terrorized the feeding station. We saw signs of foxes and Rub disappeared. Feral cats need regularity of schedule for feeding, and whether Rub moved on to a new home the human never knew. Over the months that followed, the human reported he would see my mate Scar and Copper and feed them, but the environment was too hostile for me and my new kitten to be returned to the wild. About a year later, the human reported that Copper and her father had moved back across the busy road to avoid the people and predators. The human didn't see them, except once a month, but he kept feeding at the usual spot out of his love for me and my family.

In time, the human moved Grace and me to a larger room and then introduced us to Park, Leo, and Tiny. Park and Leo readily accepted us! I warmed up to my new indoor environment and enjoyed my times with Grace. I no longer had to worry about predators, getting food, avoiding people, finding shelter from the elements of nature, and protecting my kittens from other cats. The human didn't want to rob me of my heritage and my outdoorsy wit. He slowly introduced Grace and me to the outside woods in small thirty-minute time frames. Grace went crazy with all of the new things to investigate, but I slowly investigated every tree, every bush, and any structures within thirty yards. When I felt it was safe, I lay in the sun with one eye always on Grace. The human told me I was an excellent mother.

My friendship and trust of the human grew. I allowed him to pick me up, pet me, and kiss me. He loved me very much, and always shared with me every time he saw any member of my family. The human was very patient. He knew it was difficult to see a feral cat become a domesticated cat. Park, Grace, and I became great friends. We slept together occasionally, but usually it was Grace and me sleeping together. (See picture next page.) The human loved me unconditionally. I was very grateful for his words of affirmation. He continually told me I was an excellent mother. I tried to be the best mother I could be. I had really changed since I met the human. I now trusted him and even purred whenever he touched me. His gentle touch of love and mercy resulted in me purring in the ears of God!

Life Values and Lessons from Callie

1. An excellent mother has worth far above jewels, gold, and silver. She makes sacrifices of herself and her time, as well as making the best of difficult situations for the sake of her family. She is to be admired and appreciated. Today, tell your mother how thankful you are for all she has done for you.

2. Even the best mother in the world needs divine help. She cannot do it all. She will be involved in some life and death situations as Callie was. If it had not been for the divine intervention of another, Callie and her kitten Grace would not

have survived. God knows the unique needs of all mothers, children, and fathers, and He is waiting for us to call on Him alone for strength, wisdom, and direction. Mothers try to sleep with one eye on their children to watch over them and protect them, but God never sleeps or grows tired. His eyes see it all. His ears hear it all. His foreknowledge knows what could and will happen before it does. He is never surprised!

3. Changes in a family can be disturbing and challenging! Callie experienced changes with additional kittens, the loss of kittens, a hard labor, location changes, and health problems. Every family has some difficult transitions to work through. God never intended us to work through difficulties alone. He is an ever-present help in tight places and always available to help. May we allow Him to help in the tough times as well as the good times!

4. People are not cats and cats are not people. Cats purr in our laps or in passing affection touches. It is purring that reaches God's ears! On the other hand, we can offer praises and thanksgiving to God for His faithfulness in our life and the opportunities for another day. When we do this, it is like purring in God's ears as well.

CHAPTER 9
Tuffy

THE CAT THAT
WAS GENTLE

My name is Tuffy and I am probably the oldest cat in the whole park. I keep to myself mostly and nobody knows me except the human. Even the maintenance people from the park don't know who I am. I am a stealth cat and one that reveals himself to no one but the human. The human named me Tuffy because of all the tough experiences I had been through. The human appreciated that despite my circumstances I remained gentle, shy, and not bitter.

I had lived in the park for about nine or ten years. Part of the reason I had survived for so long is that I adjusted to change and the human provided for me. For years, I lived in the swimming pool pump house. The only time I came out was at night to scrounge for food in trashcans around the marina and the golf course. When that didn't yield results, I would hunt moles, squirrels, and mice. The swimming pool was fenced so it was a safe haven from predators, such as foxes. During the evening hours, I ran into my friend Charlie, who had been trapped, spayed, left ear tipped, and then released back to her territory around the golf clubhouse. We buddied around and hunted together some. Winters were always the toughest to survive. During one of those winters, Charlie and I looked for some food around one of the trashcans late at night. The human saw us, talked softly to us, and left some food for us. He came back the next night and left us dry and wet cat food mixed. Every night, rain or shine, the human showed up and provided food for us at the golf clubhouse. I was leery and stayed back, but Charlie was always hungrier than I was and she would move toward the food first. Over time, the human left canned milk mixed with water. That was the best! The human was never pushy and always very patient. He petted Charlie while she drank the milk. When it rained or snowed, the human fed us on a corner of the porch of the old golf clubhouse so that we could eat and stay dry. The human was always thinking of us!

The first major trauma I experienced came about a year or two after the construction began on a new golf clubhouse. The new clubhouse was built farther from the woods and put Charlie and me at risk of being seen. In addition, the old clubhouse was destroyed so we had no safe place to feed. The human found other places to feed us, but they were not protected. The second major trauma I experienced was when I lost my longtime friend Charlie. She didn't die, but she followed someone home from the golf course. She never came back. The human told me Charlie found a new home. I was glad for Charlie, but I was terrified and very lonely. Occasionally, raccoons or foxes ate the food at the feeding place on the edge of the woods, and I would have to go hungry. When the human didn't see me at the feeding station, he would whistle for me to come to another place close to the marina. On another occasion, the foxes staked out the usual feeding station for about a week or more. I was petrified and hid in a hole next to a marsh. The human found me there and fed me. He was always looking out for me.

The worst trauma occurred about a year after they closed the swimming pool and destroyed my home at the pumping station. This forced me to look for a new home again. In that chaos, the human still came every night. He whistled and hollered my name. He wanted to feed me. I was comforted to know someone cared for me even when I didn't show up for weeks! The human was always looking for different places to feed me: under big trees, under a park bench, or on a tile next to a parking lot. He would still bring the canned milk and cat food. About six months after the fox incident, another traumatic situation arose. A mean rogue named TJ showed up. He would commandeer my feeding station, but the human encouraged me to eat elsewhere or he would watch over me while I ate. From what the human told me, TJ treated all the other park cats the same. He intimidated them. Sometimes he beat them up and controlled their feeding station. He didn't have a heart of a cat—he was a greedy pig. The human used his spotlight and his German Shepherd to help keep TJ in his place. Other times, when TJ was at the feeding station, the human would leave, hoping TJ would move since TJ would try to hit seven feeding stations every night to exalt his prowess. The human agonized over the damage TJ was doing. On one such occasion, TJ and I got in a scuffle. TJ had some cuts and wounds, but my front left leg was injured in the combat. I was hurt bad enough that I didn't show up to eat for several nights. When I finally felt well enough to go out, I limped on three legs. When the human saw me hobbling around, he knew I was in trouble. No cat on three legs could escape from foxes, raccoons, or other predators. My days were limited. The human came up with a plan. He told me to stay safe and he would return the next night with a solution. I had no idea of what that would be!

The next night he showed up with a trap. He covered the trap with a small blanket and placed my usual food in the trap. I was extremely leery but more hungry than suspicious since I had eaten only once in the past week. He calmed me down by putting my milk out and some dry food. Then he left to take care of the other cats. When he came back thirty minutes later, I was in the trap. My stomach was full but my nerves were frazzled. I had no idea what was going to happen next. He took me to his home and the next morning to the vet. I was a wreck until he spoke in soothing tones and told me he was trying to get me help for my leg as quickly as possible. The vet cleaned my wounds and doctored them with medicine. He informed the human how bad the wound was and that I had already been neutered. The human was shocked and quickly understood my trust issues. He realized my first trauma was when someone dumped me off in the park eight years before. After the vet was finished doctoring me, the human took me to his home and confined me in a small room with food, warmth, and milk. He came in, talked with me, and rubbed my head. I was upset from being caged and taken to the vet so I hissed at him. My fussing didn't faze him. He was not offended or scared because he understood I had experienced a tougher life than he ever imagined. The human vowed to make it as easy as he could by returning me to my familiar territory. He was determined to capture and relocate TJ. I had experienced a tough life, but it would have been even tougher if the human had not intervened on my behalf. I looked forward to my release and a stronger bond with the human in the days to come. I had not purred once for him since he caught me in the trap, but I realized I had something to purr about since I knew he was my friend forever!

About five days after my capture, true to his word, the human released me back to my home. When he let me go, I didn't run away. I stopped and listened to his voice. He fed me once again and talked to me. We bonded for about thirty minutes. When we parted, I knew the human loved me unconditionally!

Every evening, he continued to show up. I ran to him and talked to him. I was as excited to see him as he was to see me. I know there may be other traumas, but I'm confident the human will be there for me to help me. My name may be Tuffy because of all the tough circumstances I faced in my life, but my heart is tender and gentle despite my rough and tumble beginnings. The love of the human brought out the gentleness in my heart and has changed my purr forever!

Life Values and Lessons from Tuffy

1. Sometimes life can bring a parade of troubles. It may deal us one traumatic experience after another, as portrayed by Tuffy being dumped in a park, having his homes destroyed several times, losing his only friend, and being bullied. Such difficulties can toughen or harden the heart. Yet through it all, Tuffy maintained a tender heart and gentle spirit. The human understood Tuffy's pain, and Tuffy's heart was comforted and

strengthened because the human understood! Likewise, our Father in heaven knows and understands our tough times. He divinely uses those difficult moments in our lives to propel us toward Him and develop a gentleness of heart and spirit within us.

2. When Tuffy did not show up for his feeding, the human searched for him, calling his name and whistling for him day after day. He never gave up. When Tuffy finally showed up, the human rejoiced and was very thankful. Our Father in heaven searches for the lost and hurting. When they are found, there is much rejoicing in heaven.

3. Many of us will experience a life-threatening injury like Tuffy did. Without quick divine intervention, we would be vulnerable to predators and the elements of life. We should give thanks for those who intervened quickly on our behalf and look compassionately for the opportunity to help someone else. Then we won't have regrets that we didn't act quickly enough to aid those in distressing situations.

4. The tough times Tuffy went through were responsible for the close relationship and unique bonding he shared with the human. We should allow God to use our tough experiences to bond us with Him forever. When we do, they will enrich our relationships with others and give us a compassionate and gentle spirit. In that way, the product of all of those tough experiences is not bitterness that destroys but a gentleness and meekness, encouraging us and all those around us.

CHAPTER 10

Copper

THE CAT THAT
WAS THE LEAST

Sometimes in a family there is a pecking order—firstborn jockeying for position over second-born and last-born. Even with twins, this sibling rivalry can exist. My name is Copper and I am a beautiful soft golden-colored cat. I seem to be the least of Callie's kittens. I was born at the same time as Rub and Splotchy, but being least was my perception! Maybe my actions reinforced that notion because I was always the one that stayed back in the woods while the others interacted with the human. As soon as he stepped back, I would hustle to the food and gobble it up as quickly as I could. I loved the milk and food he provided. He always gave us just the right amount. I loved the night trips to the feeding station along the lake. But it seemed I was always the last to get attention or play with the rest of the family. However, the human said my name and tried to give me a special portion of milk. I may have been the least in Callie's family, but the human saw me very differently.

Things were going along smoothly until my mother, Callie, announced she was pregnant again. She refused to go to the feeding station at night because she had gained a lot of weight and was in pain. It was too difficult for her to get around. I realized things weren't going well for my mother hen she stopped playing with us. One morning when I woke up, she was gone. Rub and I looked everywhere for her. We meowed loudly for her, but there was no sight or sound. After looking all morning, we crept back to the feeding station. The smell of Callie, a smell of death, and lastly the smell of the human were all there. We could not understand the events. Rub and I didn't stay long but quickly retreated to our safe zone.

That night Rub was hungry and wanted me to go with him to the feeding station, but we had never gone there without our mother, Callie. We felt as if we were children crossing the street the first time without an adult. I was scared, but Rub went ahead. When Rub got back, he shared a fantastic story. He told how the human was there with food and milk and how the human had told him that Callie had some serious problems giving birth to the other kittens. There were stillborns, and she had lost so much blood she went into shock. We were glad to know our mother, Callie, was getting the medical attention she needed. The human promised to return her to the colony if he could. Hunger pangs drove Rub and I back to the feeding station, and on our return, there was the human with food and milk. He faithfully came every night! One night, he brought Callie and my new baby sister Grace in a cage. We could see the human's heart of compassion and that he was trying to return our mother to us.

In the weeks that followed, disaster struck! Raccoons had taken over our feeding station and chased us away. On a couple of occasions when the raccoons weren't there, a coyote showed up. Our mother had taught us how to hunt for food, but it was going to be hard to be on our own. Rub and I were thankful we had each other to face this fight! Just when things couldn't get any worse, Rub never returned from one of his hunting expeditions. This had happened before for a few days, but this time it was permanent. Whether Rub was killed by a predator or finally found a "forever" home where someone else would take care of him, I didn't know. I hoped he was safe and sound in a new home, but now I was alone and I was petrified!

I revisited the feeding station a few times and was thankful to see the human had left a feast for me. One of those times, the human was there. He tenderly spoke my name. After he fed me royally, he explained what had happened at the feeding station. He knew there was serious trouble because he had seen the tracks of the raccoons and coyote. The human knew he couldn't release Callie and Grace into that hostile environment or they would be killed. I understood the situation was very dangerous and I was alone. It is almost impossible to relocate feral cats since we are very territorial. I remembered that my mother, Callie, had moved us when we were young because foxes were hunting close to our safe zone. She took us safely across a busy road into a rock den, which had an entrance and an exit that was predator proof. There were several such rock dens because of a quarry that had been in the area years before. We could see the feeding station from the entrance to some of the rock dens. The only disadvantage to the location was that we had to cross a busy road, go under the road in a drainage pipe, or go the longer way under a bridge. That way was safer from cars and moving vehicles but more dangerous because of the people.

When I moved across the road, I found my father hunting there and some other stray cats, one named Smudge. Life there was not a perfect existence, but we were safe and that brought peace of mind. We had to work hard at finding food. Sometimes on a still night I could hear the faint whistle of the human at the feeding station. On one occasion, I shot across the road and the human recognized me immediately even though we had not seen each other for months. He was excited to see me and called me by name. That night I ate very well. A few weeks later, I went around the long way under the bridge and approached the feeding station from a different direction. The human was waiting for me again. He called me by name, talked with me, and served me a meal fit for a queen.

One night I was sitting outside my den in the quarry with a view of the feeding station a hundred yards away. I heard the human whistle and call my name. I peeked out the entrance of our home and noticed the human shining a bright light in a circle around the feeding station, checking for predators. He was also trying to find us. When the spotlight flashed in my eyes, the human spoke my name tenderly. He knew I wouldn't cross the road until the traffic died out. He was never pushy! His unconditional love and concern for me thrilled my heart. I may be the least in the eyes of others, but I was the greatest cat in the human's eyes. Maybe one day I will let him pet me and I will purr for him like Callie and my brother Rub did. It may take some time, but the human seems to give freely of his time and is patient toward us unwanted cats.

Life Values and Lessons from Copper

1. Sometimes, people's birth order can affect them for their entire life, particularly if they suffer from feelings of inferiority. Many times those who feel they don't measure up or think they are the least may be at a great advantage of being comforted by their heavenly Father because their hearts may be more sensitive to the things of God. Of course, being the least could lead to always trying to prove themselves as better or equal with everyone else, which has a tremendous downside and negative connotations. If people suffer from inferiority, their heart moves toward humility, but if they are caught in the tangled web of trying to prove their worth, their hearts can move toward pride. When we study Copper's life in the woods, there is a great sense of elegance in her demeanor. She moved toward humility and dependence on the human. Her behavior mirrors how God wants us to depend on Him for our sense of worth. Which way is your heart leaning?

2. Just as we cannot control our birth order, we have no power over some of the difficult circumstances that come our way. Copper could not control the loss of her mother, the breakup of her family, the destruction of her feeding station, and all the turmoil that followed. It wasn't her fault, and there was nothing she could have done to prevent it. Likewise, we need to learn to put difficulties behind us and press on to know the

Omniscient God who will use it all for our good as well as the good of others.

3. In the midst of turmoil, confusion, and extreme misfortune, the God of the Universe is still ever there, loving and providing for us. We may not sense His presence in everything we do, but sometimes we need to return to the last place we heard His voice. When we do, we will realize that He is ever looking for us, providing for us, and desiring our best.

4. The unconditional love of God, no matter whether we are the least or the greatest, the ugliest or the most beautiful, the dumbest or the smartest, the poorest or the richest, and so forth, is overwhelmingly sufficient for our greatest need if we would just grasp it and never let go. In this story, the unconditional love of the human is evidenced by his continual provision, concern, and availability for Copper even when she could not see it. We too miss these unseen displays of God's unconditional love. May we have eyes to see it!

CHAPTER 11

Grace

THE CAT THAT WAS
MOST FORTUNATE AND BLESSED

Of all of the feral cats in this book, the human told me that I, Grace, was the most fortunate. Without divine intervention in my circumstances, I wouldn't be bringing smiles and great joy to the human who rescued me and my mother, Callie. My mother would have died during my birth, and I would have not survived either. I never knew the hardships of scrounging for food, escaping from predators, going days without a meal, experiencing the heat of the summer and the cold of winter, knowing the dislike or hatred of people for cats, and living for fear of what tomorrow would bring. There's no doubt about it. I was a very fortunate and blessed cat. Here is my story!

My recollections of my birth and the pain my mother went through when she had me are non-existent, except for the stories the human has shared with me. He told me my siblings all were stillborn or lived only a few minutes. He also shared the veterinarian was able to save only me. My earliest memories are living in a small crate in a five-by-five foot bathroom with my mother. I slept very close to her and didn't wander from her sight. Occasionally, the human would come into the room, call my name, pick me up, and love on me. He never held me very long but always made it a point to say my name and caressed me on the head and back. My mother, Callie, would get a little anxious when the human picked me up, but when she saw how gentle he was with me, she would relax. Deep in her heart, she knew he had our best interests at heart. He was very kind and never pushy! After staying in this small room for a few months, he opened the door and allowed us to investigate our new world for short periods of time. My mother was always very cautious and shuddered every time she saw me climbing up the stairs and checking out the rest of the house, but I loved adventure and enjoyed playing with toy mice. I'll never forget when I met Park and Tiny. Park was a little apprehensive about being my friend, but I eventually won him over and he would play with me. Every evening, the human placed us back in the bathroom for our own safety.

As I grew bigger, the human gave us more freedom. He opened the front door and allowed me to investigate the outside world. I thought I had died and gone to cat heaven. There were bugs, flowers, trees, bushes, grass, and plenty of room to go exploring. My mother was curious about our new surroundings and investigated the premises with me. She kept a close eye on me. I had the time of my life scampering up trees and playing hide and seek with the human and Park. There was a very large Norway Spruce about forty feet high that my mother and I discovered about thirty feet from the front door. My mother, Callie, used this large tree to teach me how to climb and how to run to safety when a dog came or something unusual occurred.

During these outings I was also introduced to Leo, Asa, and Cassidy. The human was always watching to make sure nothing happened to me. He also made sure the other cats knew this was going to be my new home. These outings started during the daylight hours and occasionally we had a few outings at night. I treasured these times of being curious and playing. When we were finished, the human placed us in the bathroom and fed us.

Since I was getting bigger, the human moved my mother and me to a large bedroom. He supplied us with plenty of toys, food, water, and kitty litter. My mother was always by my side, whether we were inside or outdoors. Occasionally, the human would pack my mother and me in a carrier and take us to the pier to see Rub and Copper. I felt kind of sad they were more interested in food than getting re-acquainted. The human had planned on releasing my mother and me back at the pier, but a crew of raccoons tore up the feeding station and intimidated the other cats. Then one day, a coyote was sighted in the area so the human realized it would be extremely difficult to release us back into the wild. About this time, somebody came to the human's home to pick up some donations. This person saw me and picked me up. There was talk of letting this person adopt me, but the human realized the dependency between my mother and me was so great that the shock of the adoption might emotionally harm my mother. I was glad he made this decision because I really loved my new home!

As my mother and I became accustomed to the territory and safe havens around the house, the human allowed our outings outside to last longer. One day we discovered a cat door. We could go through that door and go outside any time we pleased. I was young and frisky, but Park was very gentle and gracious with me. He allowed me to follow him around to understand our boundaries and danger points. There were woods, a dry creek bed, plenty of birds and squirrels, a fishpond, and gobs more territory to explore. Life here was never boring! The human frequently picked me up and took me inside so I wouldn't get too tired. I really didn't want to slow down. I was so excited, and life was so much fun!

The human tucked me in the safe room at night. He knew I was not woods smart like the other cats. It would take time for me to realize there were predators and hurts in the real world that I was not prepared for yet, especially at night. I remember one night in my nearby wanderings, I ran across another feral cat named Cougy. He surprised me and chased me up a tree. I heard the human calling and whistling for me, and I could see the other cats looking with him, but I had been so scared by the encounter I stayed in the tree until morning. When he came looking for me again, the human told me Leo had several face-offs with Cougy. He warned me to stay close to home for my own safety. I was convinced of the human's love for me and appreciated the boundaries he provided. He loved me greatly and hoped I would grow in much grace and purrfect knowledge!

Life Values and Lessons from Grace

1. The beginnings of life can be very tough, cruel, and extremely overwhelming. Problems are out of control, and we cannot resolve them. This was very true for Grace! She had no control over the circumstances of her birth and was unable to solve her family's problems. She was the last-born, but in the sovereignty of God she was not only fortunate but her future was blessed. Likewise, we need supernatural insight from God to see our good fortune and blessings no matter whether we had tough times at the beginning, in the middle, or toward the end of our journey here on earth. The purpose of those tough times is to teach us extreme dependence on God and His Son.

2. Grace was blessed by the protection she received from her mother, her mentors, and the human. She was protected from physical, mental, and emotional harm. It was a protection that provided liberty within boundaries. Grace learned to enjoy the freedom within those boundaries. As she accepted her constrained freedoms, she was blessed. In contrast, unqualified freedom in any area of human activity is deadly for only God is absolutely free! As we accept the boundaries God has placed uniquely for each of us, we too will be most fortunate and blessed. Strive for those blessings in God.

3. As Grace accepted the boundaries defined by God, she enjoyed life and brought joy to others. Life was fun for her! Although there were difficulties with other cats from time to time, she had an enthusiasm about life that was contagious. Ask yourself, do you have that enthusiasm for life? If not, maybe you need a personal relationship with God through His Son. Or if not that, maybe there are events, people, or situations that have hardened or embittered your heart. Draw close to God as He draws you to Himself, and He will provide the enthusiasm about life!

CHAPTER 12
Charlie

THE CAT THAT
WANTED A HOME

My name is Charlie. I have black charcoal-colored fur. Tuffy and I are two of the oldest cats in the park. We are longtime friends, but we only see each other occasionally now. My story and Tuffy's story are strongly linked due to my willingness to take initiative. Without me, Tuffy's story would not have been written, and without Tuffy, I might have taken too many risks. Our interesting relationship led me to finding a home. Here is my story.

Like so many cats before me, I had a beautiful family and home, but when my original owner moved, I was dumped in a parking lot in a big park of about 300 acres. There were a golf course, swimming pool, tennis courts, marina, restaurant, picnic tables, and lots of people. There were also predators like foxes and raccoons. Not long after I was dumped in the park, someone trapped me, had me spayed, and then released me back in the park. I learned later this is called Trap, Neuter, and Release or TNR. They provided no love, no food, and no continual oversight. This was my second contact with people, and I was not impressed. Hanging around them had not been pleasant. The strange thing was, even though I never felt comfortable around people, I still craved love and a home I could call my own!

Since I was dumped in the parking lot, I roamed the outskirts of the lot, which was bordered, by woods, a marsh, a golf course, and a swimming pool. Usually I stayed within a hundred yards of the golf clubhouse since there were a number of safe zones from the foxes. On one of my night excursions, I came across Tuffy, who lived in the swimming pool area. We decided to hunt together since foxes would frequently try to team up on one cat at night, and there was safety in numbers. Sometimes we were successful, and other times we would go days without food. I had figured out how to get in the covered trashcans so I would climb in and bring some leftovers or trash out and share with Tuffy. However, this was always our last resort for food. Winter was always the most difficult time to find food since the trashcans were not used very much. Tuffy and I would spend a lot of time hunting mice in the high grass around the marsh. Once we got a meal, Tuffy would return to his swimming pool pump house, and I would hide around the edge of the golf course garage. It was a tough existence as food seemed to drive everything we did, but Tuffy and I survived even though we were severely underweight.

One winter evening, the human who walked in the park spotted me. I dropped back in the shadows and watched as the human quickly left. A few minutes later he appeared with food for me. He placed my supper on the porch of the golf house. My tummy was full from eating so well! The next night he returned with food again, but Tuffy was with me. I didn't know if he would have food for two hungry cats, but he fed us both. On some nights, he brought us a delicious drink of diluted canned milk. It was very rich. All winter, the human fed us every night. I trusted him more every time he fed me. I would inch my way closer and closer to him. I meowed loudly before he fed me. I just wanted him to know I was hungry. Then I meowed loudly after I ate the scrumptious meal he provided to let him know I was thankful for the food. He spoke our names often, but he was never pushy. He fed us and backed away, giving us plenty of room to eat without pressure. Tuffy lingered back as I moved toward the human, but soon he realized the human loved us unconditionally.

His love for us was tested when spring came and chaos began. The golf clubhouse was torn down, and a new one was built farther away from the woods. The human had a hard time finding a safe dry place to feed us. Our feeding station was always changing. It was either under a tree, under a picnic table, or under a bush. We were always looking over our shoulder worried that another cat, a raccoon, or a fox might come out of the woods and take our food away. We were always thankful when the human stood and watched us while we ate. When the swimming pool was torn down, Tuffy lost his home. We were surrounded by change and couldn't even sleep in the same place every night. To say the least, it was very difficult not having a place to call home. Some nights Tuffy and I were so stressed by the events of the day we weren't near the latest feeding station and another animal got to our food before we did. That happened a lot! We went days without food other than what we foraged for ourselves from the marsh or in the woods.

Sometimes the human wasn't able to come to our feeding time, so he sent one of his helpers to feed us. We kept our distance from the helpers even though they fed us the same food as the human. Tuffy had been through so much change he always stayed in the shadows, but I knew if the helper had been sent by the human, then there should be no fear. One night I followed one of the helpers who lived on the edge of the park. The home of this helper had no raccoon or fox problems because of all of the dogs. I enjoyed camping out at the helper's house. I was fed and cared for. Occasionally, I would go back and visit with Tuffy, but I knew it was much safer at the helper's house. One day the human showed up with a shelter for me to live in. He called my name and fed me just like old times. The helper fed me twice a day. This was a huge improvement, because I was fed only once a day at the park and the food is great! I found the home I had always dreamed of. All the love, provision, and protection fit me "purrrr"fectly! Best of all, I could travel back to the park and visit with my friend Tuffy.

I wish my story ended here, but life can change at any moment. The human's helper became critically sick and eventually his house was foreclosed. I was homeless again, but the human showed up and fed me. As I ate, he encouraged me not to lose hope. He believed I would live in a forever home soon!

Life Values and Lessons from Charlie

1. Charlie was a throwaway! She was a statistic—a homeless cat longing for love. And yet, Charlie persevered where she was. She developed a great friendship with Tuffy, and she met the human, who cared for her and eventually was responsible for Charlie finding a home. It is extremely difficult when people treat others as dispensable or throwaway and have blatant disregard for the sense of belonging that all of us need. Rest assured that God sees it all, and He will draw us to Himself. He is all we need! As we respond positively to His drawstrings of love, we will know the depths of His mercy and His provision for our deepest needs.

2. What a chaotic time Charlie and Tuffy had when all that was safe and familiar to them was destroyed. Surviving one more day was their daily goal. The obvious point to be made is that we all, no matter our age, will have times that seem to be filled with chaos and tremendous needs. God is sufficient for such times, and He alone can sustain us through them. Look to Him, His word, and His Son by faith, and the chaotic times will soon have purpose.

3. If the chaotic time had not occurred, Charlie would have been too comfortable and would have missed what God had for her. Chaos may be very stressful and extremely uncomfortable, but it is necessary to make us willing to go the way God desires for us to go. The end result for Charlie was a blessing, and the end result for us will also be a blessing.

4. Finally, Charlie's greatest desire was a home filled with love and a place to belong. In the final scheme of things, the eternal home filled with love is in heaven with God and His Son for those who know Jesus Christ as their Savior. We hope and pray to see you there!

Prologue

Each chapter has a cat story that is unique, simple, and powerful in illustrating truth. Some of these stories are continuing on. I have my favorites, as I'm sure you will too. I have lived and experienced every situation with these cats. In fact, I'm confident our sovereign God will take most of us through these various circumstances so He might conform us to the image of Christ and so our trust will be in Him and His Word and not in ourselves or institutions. It took years for these cats to trust their caretaker, and God knows it takes time as well for our trust in Him to be molded and increased. God is very patient, loving, all knowing, and ever present for us each day. He is continually drawing us to Himself, His thoughts, and His ways. His gentle wooing charms our hearts. Difficult times and hard situations are necessary to make us teachable and extremely dependent on Him. The end result is glory to God, and a greater knowledge of Him, and a stronger relationship with the God who created all that is in this world. May your intimacy with God and His Son excel to the point that you too will be able to "purr" in His ears every day.

The following list of verses by chapter is just a starting point of references for the concepts and truths embodied in each story and highlighted at the end of each chapter. Enjoy the wonderful discovery of knowing God . . . for He already knows you!

1. Blondie: The Cat that Lost What He Had – Philippians 3:8-11; Matthew 13:45-46

2. Goldie: The Cat that Wanted a Friend – 2 Chronicles 20:7; Isaiah 41:8; 1 Samuel 20:12-17; Proverbs 17:17; John 15:13-15

3. Sandy: The Cat that Nobody Wanted – Luke 17:11-19; 13:10-17

4. Park: The Cat that Was Mistreated – Luke 6: 27-36; 18:31-34; 1 Thessalonians 2:2; Acts 7:2-6

5. Tiny: The Cat that Was a Mistake – Romans 8:28; Judges 11:1-33

6. Leo: The Cat that Had a Hard Life – James 1:2-4; Romans 5:1-6; John 16:33

7. Cord: The Cat that Was Bullied – Philippians 2:3-5; Galatians 6:2-5; James 2:8; 3:13-18

8. Callie: The Cat that Was a Mother of Excellence – Ruth 3:11; 2 Samuel 21:7-14; Proverbs 31:10-31

9. Tuffy: The Cat that Was Gentle – Psalms 18:35; Ephesians 4:1-6; Colossians 3:12-17

10. Copper: The Cat that Was the Least – Luke 9:46-48; Matthew 19:30

11. Grace: The Cat that Was Most Fortunate and Blessed – Psalm 32:1-2; 33:12; Matthew 5:3-11; Ephesians 1:3; James 1:2

12. Charlie: The Cat that Wanted a Home – 2 Corinthians 5:6-9; Psalm 68:5-6